AMAZON FBA

A STEP-BY-STEP GUIDE TO PRIVATE LABEL & BUILD A SIX-FIGURE PASSIVE INCOME SELLING ON AMAZON.

JONATHAN BECKER

TABLE OF CONTENTS

INTRODUCTION

Fulfillment by Amazon also called FBA - is a process whereby sellers send their products to Amazon and leave the organization to advance those products, take payment and satisfy orders, handle most interchanges with enquirers and buyers and in this way send a segment of cash back to the seller.

Amazon FBA, is the open door it provides, regardless of how much or little you need to make and contribute. You can start up your FBA business with only a couple of hundred dollars, and still make a tidy profit. You can develop it gradually, or you locate an excellent money-spinner and contribute more. It's everything down to you.

Amazon is an ace of web trade and has set the bar high for their customers, sellers, and proprietors. Customer service is necessary for them, and we are taking advantage of this utilizing Fulfillment by Amazon. You as the product seller never again need to manage the customer service after the deal. You essentially continue sending more products to Amazon, and they deal with the rest. Amazon is among the most prominent and most well-known internet shopping sites.

CHAPTER ONE

AMAZON FBA

What is Amazon FBA?

As a business proprietor or person who is hoping to sell products using Amazon, having the chance to exploit Fulfillment By Amazon can be very helpful. With the capacity to limit the measure of time that you would spend selling and shipping your products, Fulfillment By Amazon does the more significant part of the work for you. In case you're presently inspired by these services, beneath is data and how it very well may be useful for your selling needs.

The Fulfillment Process

The whole process is generally straightforward. You will be given a chance to store your products in one of Amazon's fulfillment focuses. When a customer buys something that you have available to be purchased, they will pick, pack, and ship it for you. Additionally, customer service will be dispensed to every product that you are hoping to sell. That implies that if your buyer has any inquiries, customer service will deal with the questions.

Charges

Another considerable benefit related to utilizing Amazon FBA is that you will have the capacity to exploit their services for a negligible charge. As a more savvy arrangement than opening your warehouse and pressing/shipping your goods, you can dispose of this tedious assignment without paying ludicrous expenses. You will have the capacity to pay as you go when you begin working with Amazon. Each organization will be charged by the space that you use in the warehouse and the measure of orders that Amazon satisfies.

What to Sell Using Amazon FBA

One of the highest points of interest related to utilizing Amazon's Fulfillment to sell your goods is that many distinctive categories told you what to sell. The more significant part of sellers lists their products in the "Open Categories" segment because of the way that listing products under these categories do not require approval. A portion of the Open Categories accessible to organizations include:

· Amazon Kindle

· Books

· Baby Products

· Cameras and Photos

· Cell Phones

· Home and Garden

· Accessories for Electronics

Alternate categories accessible for people pondering what to sell utilizing Amazon FBA are known as "Proficient Seller Categories." To list your products, you will require approval. A portion of these categories include:

· Automotive and Powersports

· Beauty

· Collectible Coins

· Clothing and Accessories

· Fine Art

· Gift Cards

· Grocery and Gourmet Food.

These are only a couple of accommodating tips and indications to help you as you push ahead with your fulfillment business.

You may have found out about FBA on numerous sites, particularly on Amazon. FBA .

Would you be able to set aside extra cash or appreciate different benefits with this offer or process? If you are searching for answer to these inquiries, you are on the correct page.

The organization gets payments for each order put on the web and the conveys the required goods to every buyer.

With the assistance of this process, a lot of stores have appreciated a suitable arrangement of development in their deals. A few stores have Amazon finish the orders for goods. Regularly, the products are explicitly sent to the buyers by the sellers selling straightforwardly on Amazon. Now and again, it occurs by the sellers on different sites, for example, Etsy, eBay that moves to the FBA. Thus, it's fascinating to know how this offer by the vast store has benefited people everywhere throughout the world.

As indicated by numerous sellers, they have encountered a vast ascent in their business volume. Then again, buyers trust that they are obtaining from a commendable trust organization rather than a person. Purchasing straightforwardly through FBA adds to the trust of the buyer in the provider. Along these lines, they may buy again not far off.

Beside this, sellers can influence the use of this offer

to accomplish numerous different benefits. If you use this service as a seller, you won't need to stress over the advancement of the product. Also, it will be Amazon's obligation to manage buyers and satisfy orders. Then, you can concentrate on different undertakings, for example, getting new products and do different assignments that may make your business considerably greater.

Extra benefits:

You are a product proprietor; you can take some days off without agonizing over who will deal with your business while you away. Your business will continues running while you are have time with your companions in Paris. Along these lines, you can avoid your office for the same number of days as you needed. Whatever length of time that Amazon has products in their stock, you are a great idea to go, and you don't have to stress over anything.

A few people don't prefer to manage buyers straightforwards. They think that it's difficult to manages troublesome customers. These things will be dealt with by Amazon.

You don't know anything about FBA yet, realize that figuring out how to use it isn't hard in any way. You can go to the official site of Amazon to download the pdf archives to find out about how to begin. Inside a couple of minutes, you will be comfortable with the entire framework.

Along these lines, if you have your store, you can benefit from this extraordinary service offered by Amazon.

Simple Start With Amazon FBA!

Amazon made many refer to as Fulfillment By Amazon which works a lot like eBay, yet is MUCH better.

For some time, eBay was the central place to sell things on the web. eBay is extraordinary, yet it requires a lot of work on your part: sourcing, posting, shipping, customer bolster and so on.

If you plan to sell to on the web, you ought to unequivocally consider Amazon's fulfillment program called FBA. What makes FBA much more unprecedented is that its items are additionally qualified for Amazon's shipping advancement including Free Super Saver Shipping and Amazon Prime.

How FBA works and how different businesses are utilizing FBA.

Amazon purchasers utilize Prime, so they get free shipping. They effortlessly spend more on things like flavors, espresso, tea, socks, tissue, towels, cleanser, and so forth. They pay considerably more since they entirely TRUST Amazon. This is useful for sellers since it implies that you will make increasingly and sell more.

This will cover just setting up your Amazon accounts for FBA. We will go more into send your products to Amazon, putting away and shipping your products on Amazon.

1. Open an Amazon Account

You have never obtained nor sold on Amazon and don't have an account, go to the Amazon website and tap on the Selling on Amazon connect at the base of any page.

2. Set Up Your Amazon Account

When you have an Amazon selling account, contact the Amazon customer service division to set up your account for FBA. Having a good FBA rep on your account will assist you with any issues later on. The rep will walk you through your first shipment.

So if you get this far, you have done your underlying due determination, and you have an FBA account.

Fulfillment By Amazon is a program set up by Amazon that enables you to utilize Amazon to the stockroom and after that convey your items (and furthermore dependably you to sell your questions on the Amazon Site). Amazon FBA is extremely basic, and yet is incredible and can take your business to the following dimension for low costs.

Envision the scene you are caught up with doing your product sourcing and have picked up a few books, CD's DVD's, Home and Beauty items a couple of new toys (Yes items sold using Amazon FBA must be either new or collectible). Presently regularly at the back of your mind, you are considering; however there is no more space at home. This is the place the Amazon FBA becomes an integral factor. Also, you can test the water out of utilizing the first Amazon selling account, or you can be a Pro-Merchant, it doesn't make a difference.

You return home and output or rundown the items as common into your Amazon selling the account and a couple of snaps later, you print out some barcodes which you should put over the first barcode on the item (Yes items should have a barcode or recorded on the Amazon site). A couple of more snaps and you print out a pressing slip which goes in the crate or boxes. You at that point book a get from a transporter, and this depends on where you live and how you pay for it - every nation is unique.

Next, you finish the order and trust that the law will be

picked up and inside days your item will be in the Amazon distribution center being sold for you, and you can kick back and bank the money. Amazon FBA manages installments, shipping, and customer messages; you need to source more stock and bank the money.

Indeed there are some additional costs that Amazon charges yet these are low, and the reserve funds you make on the postage is fabulous - recollect you are utilizing Amazon's purchasing power and no more lines in Post Offices and no all the more purchasing air pocket wrap and boxes.

Something different people don't understand is that you can utilize Amazon FBA to transport out to your eBay and different purchasers. Indeed Amazon store the items, and send the details out for you. Also, for almost no cost and by and large a lot less expensive than you can do. All the estimating data can be found on your nations Amazon site. Just complete a look for Amazon FBA.

Step by step to Make Money Selling On Amazon

You may be keen on learning how to make money selling on Amazon and earn commissions for your true endeavors. Numerous internet marketers are earning significant income because of the rising popularity of the internet and online shopping. Recognizing how to make money selling on Amazon can prompt a thriving internet business.

Distinguishing how to make money selling on Amazon isn't as troublesome as you think it. How to make money selling on Amazon includes some data, and comprehension of what to complete and when? Besides, it needs a specific range of abilities to get a battle ready for action adequately. For the learners, you are required to settle on which platform you need to assemble a website. Remember that Amazon should support your site at the time you present an application for the affiliate program. In this circumstance, the ideal way is getting a useful website about the products you might want, together with some extraordinary substance. You will get affirmed immediately, and after that, you will have the capacity to sell your products using Amazon links.

Making money selling on Amazon isn't positive that troublesome; however, it necessitates you to apply some critical internet marketing standards and procedures. A portion of these would fuse watchword inquire about, building major websites, learning SEO strategies, website advancement, and numerous others. Luckily, these things are something everybody can do.

Paid advertising may convey results for you; in any case, they are costly because they are evacuated when your membership closes. Then again, Amazon SEO provides you with everlasting attention. An Amazon SEO master makes a diagram on how you can liven up the permeability of your leaning to help the activity stream to it and associate effectively with your real market.

The blasting internet marketers, the ones who recognize how to make money selling on Amazon and with other affiliate systems make them thing in like manner, i.e. Appropriate information and Excellent preparing. As a piece of all-around arranged procedure, catchphrases set your SEO drive and with the consideration easy to use; high-quality substance explicitly intended to expand your product permeability to focused clients. Productive website improvement steps are used by the Amazon SEO organizations to provide your posting most great introduction pursued by better change rate, expanded deals, and higher rankings.

WHAT IS THE AMAZON FBA PROGRAM?

Start, the Amazon FBA program speaks to Fulfillment by Amazon. Amazon's FBA program is a great open door for the massive gathering of people of business people. Particularly those that are beginning as a one-person shop. This is a service Amazon provides to allow online and disengaged sellers to send their goods to Amazon, and Amazon will pack and dispatch the products to individual customers for the wellbeing of you. You may not know how huge the Amazon business focus is if you don't visit there routinely. They have gained some astounding ground from just pitching books, to now moving practically anything.

You can participate like manner move products on Amazon and not use their FBA service, so you ship your one of kind products, yet there are various central purposes of applying the FBA system, which will spare your time and provide a more robotized business course of action.

It is much a similar service that other drop shippers provide, anyway Amazon hold your very own goods in one of their fulfillment focuses. The service will send your products at whatever point and to wherever for your advantage. This system can be moreover organized with your site to make a robotized system for transmitting Amazon your goods, and for Amazon shipping them to customers. The costs for the service are to a high degree focused, and you pay for absolute limit and shipments, at refund Amazon rates, they don't charge a charge to use the system.

So, for what reason would be a good thought for you to think about using Amazon's system?

Here are a bit of the key focuses on the FBA system:

- You can move about anything on Amazon, or through your one of a kind site and have them pack and send.

- By mechanizing your site with Amazon it infers the business can continue running on autopilot, and you can evacuate time in case you pick, and your company still limits.

- Send all your stock to Amazon, and they will manage everything, you ought to accumulate your advantages.

- Amazon is by and by outranking eBay on Alexa for action, they are an imperative contender to eBay.

- Some eBay sellers are using the Amazon FBA to ship goods sold through eBay.

For example and also books, Amazon has categories

like eBay which cover virtually anything you can consider for the home, develop, office, attire, sports, and so forth.

Because of the FBA program, and the tremendous action that Amazon produces, you could make an Amazon website, find products to move and be good to go with an online business quickly with the gadgets they provide. It is undoubtedly one of the least complicated ways to deal with begin an online store in the present time.

STEP BY STEP TO SELL ON AMAZON FOR BEGINNERS

There are a few steps to takes:

Agrees to accept Amazon Seller Account. The initial phase is to get a "seller" account from Amazon. There are two sorts of seller account - "individual" and "expert." The individual is free and enables you to "list" things which as of now exist in the Amazon inventory. You pay a little fee each time a product is sold. Proficient costs $40/mo, and has no additional "per deal" fees (albeit different fees, for example, a stocking fee and so on may apply). This is the primary account which enables you to list new things in Amazon's inventory.

Agrees to accept GS1. This enables you to create standardized identifications. They comes in two organizations - UPC (Universal Product Code) and EAN (European Article Number). While these can be purchase moderately economically ($10), Amazon, Google, and eBay unequivocally suggest utilizing GS1 for institutionalization. By using GS1, you're ready to have your products perceived by any semblance of Amazon. The drawback is the cost; however it shouldn't generally matter - we always prescribe putting aside ~$500 for administrative expenses, of which would be one's.

Makes A Legal Company (Optional) If you're hoping to set up a good FBA activity, you'll need a legitimate business (and financial balance). Aside from enabling Amazon's to open a business account it allows you to more readily oversee charges (which are famously terrible for putting your cash in an individual limit). This is anything but difficult to set up, however, you need to manage Amazon on an FBA premise as it were. If you need to move products on the framework merely, the pleasure is all mine to do it under your named.

Purchase/Build Boxed Product; You at that point need to get an arrangement of boxed forms of the product. If you make the product yourself, you need to get them into traditional boxes. Since there are such vast numbers of ways to do this, we'll only say that you should search for a boxing/printing company to deal with it for you. There are numerous skilled ones. You should likewise pursue Amazon's rules on what kinds of bundling they acknowledged.

Send Products To Amazon; Once you have the boxed products, you need to send them to Amazon. This is masterminded through the Amazon seller framework, enabling you to pick a period when the products ought to get at the Amazon distribution center. Once more, because of the dimension of variety all the while, it's best to state that you ought to pursue the Amazon rules will do it.

There's beyond what one way you can make money moving on Amazon.

Most importantly, Amazon Marketplace. Marketplace offers you a chance to move products (books as well all in all scope of things) on precisely the same page on Amazon's website where Amazon run the product themselves. So you get the opportunity to contend with them head-on, and even had a chance to rival them on price. Moving prices are settled - Marketplace isn't a sale. You can list a significant number of things for nothing however what they call a referral expense is charged on every deal. The marketplace is for both new and utilized products.

The marketplace is reasonable whether you merely need to make some extra money low maintenance, yet additionally, you need to begin an 'appropriate' independent company.

The other principal way to make money is Amazon Associates. Partners is fundamentally a member program.

How to Sell on Amazon Marketplace.

To begin with Amazon Marketplace. You don't enlist ahead of time. You can open a seller accounts when you are listing your first product.

You as of now have a buyer account on Amazon you

can add your seller account to that.

To enroll as a seller, you will require a business name, a location, a presentation name, a Mastercard and a phone contact numbers. That is all you have to begins.

Amazon site, look down the pages to 'Make Money With Us' and afterward 'Move On Amazon.' You will at that point see two options:

Move a little or move a lot? Amazon offers two section focuse into Marketplace which they casually tag as 'selling a bit' or 'selling a lot.'

Mostly a bit- is for incidental and interest sellers who hope to move under 35 items every month. It cost 86p in addition to a referral fee for every deal. You are additionally limited to the product classifications you can move in. The preferred standpoint is that it costs practically nothing to begin and no continuous charges are assuming, at first, you don't run in particular.

Selling 'a lot' is for expert sellers who hope to move more than 35 items every month. You pay 28.75 month to month settled fee and a referral fee. You can walk in all the Amazon product classes.

It isn't always feasible to list low price, low volume products as a 'move a bit' seller. To do that you should be a 'move a lot' seller! You take the 'selling a bit' course to begin with. You can generally redesign later.

Pick your option, at that point fill in the inline frame.

Genius Merchant Sellers

When you are selling 'a lot' you will likely additionally need to end up what Amazon calls a Pro Merchant Seller. Genius Merchants approach volume selling and mass listing device. There is a web interface that enable you to all the effectively deal with your product descriptions, stocks, and requests. You will likewise have the capacity to fares and imports data to and from your account.

When you get going the selling, a lot/Pro Merchant option will work out a lot less expensive and, imperatively, will enable you to take a shot at more tightly edges and make money from deals that the individuals who move only a little can't.

Amazon Marketplace Selling - How to move your products

Presently we should investigate how you put products available to be purchased on Amazon Marketplace.

The possibility of Marketplace is that you move your product on the very same page on which Amazon and some other Marketplace sellers run it.

Along these lines, first, locate the same new product

in the Amazon inventory. Utilize the 'Pursuit' instrument at the highest point of the Amazon landing page. Put in the product type and name and Amazon will naturally take you to the right page to show it.

Next, check painstakingly that the product type, brand, and model numbers or whatever Amazon founds is the right ones.

When you achieve page, you'll discover a catch called 'Move Yours Here.' Tap on it, sign in to your seller account, and you would now be able to list your product promptly.

Sell On Amazon - Sell Used Books Working From Home: What You Need To Get Started Out

Amazon Marketplace is easy. You likely as of now have the more significant part of these things available as of now. If money is tight, buy little amounts to begin (envelopes, tape, bubble wrap for shipping) to help manage amid your start-up stage. Later on, you can buy in mass and set aside extra cash. You will require:

A PC with the Internet get to - If you're perusing this, you likely as of now have your PC. You'll need it consistently at inquiring about book costs, list books available to be purchased, and check for email notices.

Shipping envelopes - Large darker manila envelopes

estimated 9" x 12" and 10" x 13" work exceptionally well to ship generally books.

Bubble wrap - Protects the books from harm in the mail. You can buy a little move of clear bubble wrap nowadays at many markdown stores for about $5 to begin. This will spare you money versus purchasing bubble wrap envelopes and help you ship things that you may end up selling on eBay or other online sellers sites.

USPS Confirmation Delivery slips - These are accessible free from your nearby Post Office. They are the green and white slips that have a strip and-stick cement toward one side. Request a heap of 50-100 to begin.

Dark ink pens - Have bounty close by for tending to bundles, Delivery Confirmation slips, shipping names and making notes for yourself.

Pencils with erasers - Many libraries and some thrift shops will experience the process of denoting within the title page with a price in pencil before their sale begins. This price is typical $1, $2, $3 - and you'll have to delete this proof you got a great take on the book when you're selling it for ten times what you paid for it!

Scissors - For trimming up mis-taped packages and

chopping down cardboard pressing defenders for supporting little booklets or soft cover books. Likewise, you'll require these to cut up the bubble wrap you will use to secure books amid shipment.

Record organizers - Use up some old manila document envelopes you would dispose of in any case if you would prefer not to buy new ones, which cost about $5 for a little bundle. Trim these into two pieces, one to secure the front of the book and one to ensure back exterior of the paper when you slide the book into the shipping envelope to give additional insurance to your bundle.

Clear hardcore shipping tape and tape weapon - You'll require the tape firearm and 2-3 moves of clear tape to begin. You can buy the little plastic tape allocators for about $3 each in case you're short on money.

Cleaning supplies-You presumably as of now have these in your kitchen: paper towels, little clean brush, warm water. Try not to utilize cleaning showers to expel stains from books or the residue covers. Most times you can put a small measure of warm water on a paper towel, swipe it over the lustrous residue covers, and reestablish a spotless sparkle to the book dust cover.

Bookshelves - Needless to state, this business stock will, in general, take up bunches of room, so put aside an extra bedroom or a cool, dry place in your home that has low stickiness, far from windows that sweat to avert harm to the paper in the books, and put resources into or fabricate some racking to hold your books.

Work Table - Yes, you can utilize your lounge area table, yet having an assigned work table like a long collapsing table that can be stowed away in a utility wardrobe is a friendly method to get a mechanical production system going for (a) posting books and (b) pressing books for shipment.

Portable Smartphone - OK, this is discretionary. Most cellphone smartphones will remove a significant piece from your month to month spending plan. When you utilize the phone's web internet browser while out shopping to pull up contending prices, you'll know for sure on the off chance that you've discovered a victor or not inside seconds, so there's no second speculating.

Account Set-Up - You will require a business checking account to have installments coordinate saved into from your book sales. Approach at your bank for a free plastic to run with the account, and you won't have to compose numerous checks out of this account. You can utilize the check card to make the buys you'll have to begin and work your bookselling business. Different business needs are:

You will require a Mastercard - You will require one

for Amazon to affirm your sellers account the day you begin (it doesn't get charged again after that).

You will require a phone number - Home number or mobile phone number that Amazon will use to send you an affirmation call or instant message to affirm your personality when setting up account (this phone number doesn't get distributed on your online customer-facing facade except if you need to put it there - and I'd prescribe against that. Your clients need to get in touch with you through email in any case).

You will require a legitimate email address - This is the place you'll send messages and get book sale notices and to check email sees in regards to returns. Getting another Gmail account, and keep your business and your private email accounts independent.

Check with your city zoning division - While it boggles a few urban communities confine home businesses, it occurs. You may require a business permit in your town. You won't have clients or provider sales reps going to your home, and except if you have UPS get expansive amounts of your books to ship to the closest 'Satisfied By Amazon' (FBA) conveyance focus, your neighbors most likely will never see you even maintain a home-based business except if you let them know.

Since you know the fundamental things you'll have to

begin selling utilized books on Amazon, it's time to get occupied with sourcing books to sell on the web. It's easy to make money when you stock up on the right sorts of books. Take as much time as necessary, consult at the best costs, and limit your buys to great condition books. Your home-based bookstore will set aside the opportunity to get ready for action, yet having the right instruments available beginning will enable you to accomplish more in less time as you figure out how to sell in the Amazon Marketplace!

Presently this is the extremely tricky thing about Amazon.

Expecting the product as of now exists in the Amazon list a listing is instant for you to utilize. You don't need to compose a description or transfer a photograph. You should state what condition your product is in (i.e., new or one of a few standard utilized stories), express the amount you have available to be purchased and fill in the price you require. Additionally, choose what postage options you need to offer. (At this stage you can likewise select whether you will send the product to another country or not.)

If you wish; you can add a many description up to 2,000 characters (not words). This will enable you to separate your product or offering from Amazon and different sellers.

Amazon will give you an outline of your listing to check and furthermore affirm what their fees will be if the item moves. In case you're content with this merely click 'Present Your Listing,' and you're off. When you've done this your item is naturally recorded until the point when it moves or for 60 days (uncertainty in case you're a Pro Merchant).

Indeed, a great many online customers utilize the site every day to buy different items. Nearly anything is promptly accessible on the website and buyers can purchase anything, and some good precedents are cell phones, TVs, smartphones some more. Such a significant number of individuals at present move their products on Amazon since they appreciate the advantage of achieving lots of forthcoming clients. Not at all like eBay, clients of Amazon are not required to put offers. Like this, the products have prices recorded in addition to an extra delivering expense. The following are helpful hints on the best way to make money selling on Amazon.

Additionally, you can peruse online aides and guidelines that make the procedure less painful. By making your seller account, you are anticipated that would list down the items you might want to move. You should remember that specific products can't be sold on Amazon. To discover more about the limitations, visit the page that harps on actualities and data. This is vital for individuals thinking about how to make money selling on Amazon.

Fees are plainly shown for sellers amid the underlying, and sellers have the option of picking between two account types. One is most appropriate for individuals who expect to move a lot of items while the other bundle is intended for sellers who plan on selling just a couple of things. In any case, fees charged shift contingent upon account type chose.

You are thinking about how to make money selling on Amazon; you will be happy to discover that the site offers an attractive open door for individuals who intend to change this into business thought. Sellers are regular take pictures of products they might want to move after which they can show them on the site. Regardless of this, sellers are required to deliver their stock to Amazon. An endless supply of the methods, Amazon will dispatch the sold products to buyers who make buys along these lines enabling sellers to monitor inventory of their products effortlessly.

There is likewise an option of selling items all alone if you wish to realize how to make money selling on Amazon. Along these lines, you would need to take photos of your product and show it in the most reasonable classification. Make sure to make a fair description of your product to make it less demanding for buyers to realize what they are obtaining. Clear explanations and excellent pictures diminish occasions where buyers return items. Besides, valuing must be done well because different sellers will likewise price their products aggressively.

One more essential point to recall concerning how to make money selling on Amazon quicker is speedy delivery. Items sold ought to in a perfect world be dispatched to the buyers inside two days. Additionally, make sure to answer quickly to messages from buyers as this will keep them from making buys from different sellers.

You Can Make Money Selling On Amazon

Selling products on any merchant site is certifiably not a straightforward errand. Along these line, if you are searching for an auxiliary salary, begin with the right vision. You intend to sell on Amazon, know the ordinary entanglements that numerous sellers experience and how you can dodge them. To succeed and turn into a best seller, realize how to make money selling on Amazon.

Find what it Takes to Become an Amazon Featured Merchant

As a merchant seller on Amazon, you will never again battle to sell products. With good criticism, it will take you only a couple of months to include here. Typically, however, Amazon won't demonstrate to you industry standards to end up a merchant seller, have the right sort of seller account, strong sales, and proper audits.

Utilize the Right Fulfillment Service

This is an essential factor in the best way to make money selling on Amazon. Give Amazon a chance to satisfy the product for you. You can dispatch out items in mass yet for individual requests, leave that to the fulfillment service. Along these lines, you will have sufficient energy to develop your business and increase sales.

Pick Products Suited for Your Business Size and Available Space

Sell products that you can without much of a stretch oversee. As a starter, you can sell products that don't require a ton of work, and as you advance further, you would now be able to wander into more excellent products.

Be Flexible with your Pricing Strategy and Promotions

Most sellers on Amazon tend to under-price products to pull in more purchasers. You can diminish prices, you need more sales or raise them by 3% or less to earn more profit.

Figure out What Your Margins Are

This is likewise an essential factor on the best way to make money selling on Amazon since when you purchase a product to sell, you have to take care of the product expense. So you set low prices, you may even neglect to pay the selling charges forced by Amazon. In this way, discover more data about the product, the expenses included, sending costs too and afterward sell the right product that will profit you.

Exploit straightforward Marketing Opportunities inside Amazon

Amazon is always trying new apparatuses that you can use to support your sales and increase your salary. Incredible outcomes will anyway rely upon the product you have picked.

Prepare for the Holidays

Amid occasions sales generally will in general increase better than expected. This can be a good time for you as an Amazon seller except if you come up short on stock. Along these lines, realize how to figure request particularly, you are selling random products. This is an incredible way on the best way to make money selling on Amazon, and you won't pass up sales that would have helped your earnings.

Make utilization of Seller Central Reports

You will discover extraordinary instruments and reports too on your seller account on Amazon otherwise called the Amazon Seller Central. Here you can follow your sales, your advancements, check your stock, explanations behind returns and discounts too. This data will enable you to conjecture future purchases and increase your salary.

Most importantly, make sure to pursue Amazon's tenets and rules while selling. Inspiring prohibited in the wake of buckling down to construct and advance yourself as a seller is hugely disappointing. This is likewise a critical viewpoint on the most proficient method to make money selling on Amazon.

AMAZON FBA WILL HELP BUILD YOUR BUSINESS

What's astounding with Amazon FBA is its versatility. As a one-person shop, you can contend with the more excellent and more settled seller. Private ventures are restricted away space and the time management to sell, rundown, make and ship orders. You can satisfy small laws (ex. 20 every day) and also the more significant orders (ex. 100,000 every day) and prosper as a more significant corporate utilizing Amazon's Fulfillment. You would now be able to deal with the expanded volume practically while managing your stock and spending you to source your product.

This will lessen the upper hand of the greater seller and empower you to make a good salary and develop as large as you want. Consider it. You merely require access to your product(s) of the decision. Amazon FBA gives a flood of pay that you can take to an unheard of level. At every fulfillment focus, (Amazon has more than 65) you are contracting at LOW rates per order a staff that deals with the order handling, shipping and customer.

The seller needs to source your product(s), spend your time preparing those items and shipping them to Amazon. A portion of the critical advantages of Amazon FBA

You approach countless Prime customers

·   Scale order taking care of and construct coordinations both on and off Amazon·

· Sell all-inclusive by utilizing the FBA send out the program to access customers comprehensively at no extra cost to you.

· Multi-Channel Fulfillment (MCF) is a discretionary program by FBA that enables you to effectively use Amazon's reality class Fulfillment Centers for your off-Amazon orders.

. What's more, take a paid get-away while FBA works for you satisfying customer orders and managing customer service.

· You approach a vast number of Prime customers

· FBA now speaks to a becoming 45% of Amazon's incomes

· Amazon Prime began in 2005

· Prime speaks to just 6% of Amazon's aggregate customers up until this point

· Prime is developing at over 20% Year Over Year

· Prime customers spend 140% more than standard Amazon Customers

· 40 % - 50 % of Amazon customers have never acquired from an outsider.

With FBA, Amazon can help enhance your online deals and keep customers glad, while sparing you profitable time so you can concentrate on developing your business.

HOW TO BOOST SALES ON AMAZON

Despite being a champion amongst the most generally perceived request we get from customers, it is difficult to reply with an only answer. That is because, lamentably, there's no charm shot, however slightly, a related arrangement of tips, systems, and philosophies that you'll need to experiment with in your Amazon seller central.

In working with numerous customers, we've watched a range of Ideas - a few works and some not - that have provoked to the sales. So we have masterminded a rundown of procedures which can help your sales on amazon.com, not every one of you may get full information as indicated by your temperament of business, some of them will move your business up.

Product Images

Pictures are necessary for driving changes as buyers need to fathom what they are buying. Preferably, views ought to be over 1000X1000 pixels with a white foundation, and the whole product must be noticeable and should take up generally 80% of the space. Pictures ought to exclude watermarks, fringes, URLs, movement, seller logos or some other content.

Product Descriptions and Bullet Points

Diverse customers are going to your product with the other need, so the shorter you are in your depictions, the more accommodating you are to the customers to choose your product. An excessive amount of data likewise drives your customer away from your page so product portrayal ought to be held under 200 words roughly. What's more, however, there is no distributed rundown, constrained HTML organizing is permitted. These configurations are altogether known to work:

Most classifications will likewise permit up to five bullet points. This ought to be abnormal state subtleties that you need to incorporate, so limit bullet points to highlights with the broadest intrigue.

Enhance your amazon seller central record SEO

And additionally seller rating and price, Amazon likewise takes a gander at keywords in the product's title to rank postings. Amazon's keyword stuffing alternative for a product's title is exceptionally reminiscent of strategies SEO offices use to send to enhance Google rankings in the mid-2000s.

With the product titles, you have a character limit of 1000 characters in each column, in which you ought to incorporate whatever number keywords as could be allowed to guarantee your product is visible. Amazon recommends including brand, portrayal, product line, material, shading, size and amount in this field.

Separate from the product title, Amazon likewise offers you to enter data into a keyword field. It's essential that it is inadequate to incorporate any keywords that you had officially utilized in the product title, as Amazon will essentially disregard this. You are permitted five keywords or keyword expressions to be entered here, so use them carefully.

Publicizing

If you are merely beginning or looking to your product before whatever number eyeballs as could be allowed to attempt Amazon supported products. This empowers your product to be shown underneath list items, in the right-hand section or on detail pages.

Marketing outside of Amazon

Although email interchanges and direct calls have a place with an old school of thought and that can lead individuals away from your Amazon Store, this doesn't mean you can't marketing individuals. You can compose Article and web journals accomplish this objective; You can focus on your pertinent class with applicable substance for nothing using Word Press. There are heaps of sites which give you a chance to welcome your customers by composing articles for nothing.

Limits

Limits assume an essential job in occupying sales diagram to an abnormal state and building a bond among seller and purchasers. Every day bargains and huge ceilings could arrive you at #1 for your product classification. This likewise open up the likelihood of showing up on the Amazon landing page under the "Hot Deals" and "New and Noteworthy" classes, which will produce large measures of activity.

Amazon seller central: Fulfillment by Amazon (FBA)

Amazon enables sellers to utilize its coordinations system to store and convey their products. Amazon stores your products in its stockroom, at that point packs and ships them and also giving the after sales cares.

Product that are offered through FBA can be sold to individuals from Amazon's Prime dependability plot. Prime customers speak to an expected 6% of purchasers; however, they purchase as much as 17% of aggregate sales.

CHAPTER TWO

ESSENTIAL ON HOW TO MAKE MONEY SELLING ON AMAZON

Since its initiation Amazon has given a stage to individuals, small organizations and retailers to move their products and make better than average pay, anyway a few people don't realize how to make money selling on Amazon. A portion of the means you can pursue to end up a first class seller in Amazon are recorded underneath.

Pursue Amazon selling standards and rules

After agreeing to accept a seller account. It is important to pursue all Amazon tenets and product rules to abstain from getting restricted. This principle can be found in the assistance area of the Amazon website.

Endeavor to be an Amazon highlighted trader

Getting the opportunity to be an Amazon highlight dealer is one way of illuminating inquiry of how to make money selling in Amazon. Although Amazon does not say the correct recipe on how one turns into a highlighted shipper, one can undoubtedly join this lofty gathering following a couple of months by having great sales and brilliant customer feedback.

Be flexible in your evaluating

Although everybody's principal point is to make the most extreme benefits, it is essential to have a viable valuing technique. Check the prices of your rivals and guarantee the price contrast edge is justifiable. In the occasion your product gets more requests, you can marginally increase the amount to augment benefits.

Comprehend Amazon expenses and fees

The most effective way on the best way to make money selling on Amazon is understanding the fees and costs included. When you purchase a product to move on Amazon, you need to price it in a way that you will take care of your expense and still make a not too bad benefit.

You can dispense with delivery fees by utilizing Fulfillment by Amazon FBA which involves sending your products to Amazon who will at that point handle the bundling and transporting to customers.

Amazon likewise charges an assortment of fees including selling and referral fees.

Exploit Amazon marketing tools

Amazon has a few marketing tools that can enable your products to get took note. A portion of this tools incorporates Listmania, Likes, and Tags.

Guarantee you have enough products to take care of market demand.

Although most sellers begin little, it is prudent to have enough product supply in the occasion you start getting more requests. This guarantees your customers don't search for options and you increase your salary.

Use Amazon seller central

The ideal way on the best way to make money selling on Amazon is to always use the central seller reports. These reports cause one to examine moves, potential customers and the adequacy of advancement and marketing.

Moneymaking in Amazon

There are numerous courtesies that Amazon brings to the table for purchasers and sellers alike. In any case, the ideal way to profit by the online retail website Amazon.com is through being a part and by knowing the distinctive ways you can make money out of Amazon.

The first and evident reason is that you have the products and they can enable you to move it on Amazon itself. Consider the possibility that you have your website. At that point, you also can have that head begin with your e-business by utilizing Amazon's 1-Click Ordering.

Likewise, through Amazon's product promotions, an expense for each snap program that features your products to a great many online customers, it's as basic as transferring your products and putting their price and voila! It's for the world to see! This program requires negligible expenses enables you to acquire activity on your site, and increases your odds of higher income, with more hits and snaps.

Your business is more service-situated than that of your products, there is additionally the component of Clickriver Ads, a site which likewise offers the collaborate of your services being advanced close by your products.

Another way to have the capacity to boost profiting in Amazon is, however, its Fulfillment by Amazon (FBA) program. Through this, you get the opportunity to store your products on Amazon's fulfillment focuses, and they can securely and individually pack and ship those products, and offer quality customer service, on your sake.

As a seller, no other site can ensure the exactness of your payments yet through Checkout by Amazon, Amazon Simple Pay, and Amazon Flexible Payments, these programs guarantee and have demonstrated misrepresentation identification and enable your customers to have the capacity to get to the most secure and confided in online payment arrangements.

Amazon has such a significant amount to offer for everybody of various foundations whether you are a creator, you can likewise profit of CreateSpace, an individual from the Amazon gathering of organizations, that gives a quick, simple and sparing way to independently publish and share your substance with potential customers on Amazon.com and different sites.

As an engineer, you can increase your site's productivity by the various programs that are offered, for example, Amazon website, Marketplace Web Services, Fulfillment Web Services, Amazon Web Services, Advertising Web Services (Product Advertising API), Amazon Flexible Payments and Mechanical Turk.

All these subsidiary programs, are in alone exertion of making your online business more exceptional, and customer benevolent, and enable engineers to produce more current and more creative ways of taking care of the company, at the snap of a catch. They incorporate every one of the tools expected to spruce up your site, up to the ways where payment can be made less demanding and more open.

There are numerous ways to make money from the online retail website and things that Amazon can offer from sprouting business visionaries to old-fashioned shippers, searching for some new way to energize their businesses.

TIPS ON HOW TO MAKE MONEY SELLING ON AMAZON

With the current financial flimsiness, such a significant number of people these days are searching for other elective ways of making money. The web gives an excellent stage for making money because there are numerous clients on the internet. Amazon is a good site for people who need to sell products on the web. So if you are thinking about how to make money selling on Amazon, just gather a few items in your home that you can never again require yet are in excellent condition and begin selling them on the web. You can likewise get them at the limited price and after that resell them.

Here are tips on the best way to make money selling on Amazon.

Items to Sell on Amazon to Make Money

Attire and Accessories

There is an incredible interest for hefty size garments, youngsters' dress, vintage attire, pants, calfskin coats, originator coats and delicate clothes on Amazon. Adornments, for example, fashioner sacks, handbags, shades, gloves, shawls, watches, ties, umbrellas, caps, belts, scarves, caps and so on., can likewise sell on Amazon.

Adornments and Crafts

Adornments can likewise bring good money, especially classical gems. One of a kind high-quality products additionally have an interest in the market. So if you realize how to make form crafts, material crafts or enlivening crafts, you can transform them into money as long as you most likely are aware of how to make money selling on Amazon.

Books

You can sell books on Amazon. You can go for anecdotal and non-anecdotal books on science, history, nautical subjects, sports and so on. Textbooks can likewise sell as their high prices, for the most part, constrain people to settle on less expensive second-hand books. Indeed, even religious and comic books can earn you good money as long as you most likely are aware of how to make money selling on Amazon.

Contraptions and Electrical Appliances

Utilized contraptions and electrical appliances can get good money if they are in good condition. If they have any minor imperfections, have them fixed before selling on Amazon. The top of the line hardware on Amazon incorporate dishwashers, TVs, PCs, computer game frameworks, iPad, iPhones, iPods, MP3 players, DVD players, and advanced cameras.

Car and Spare Parts

You can earn good money by selling vehicles and motorbikes on Amazon. You can even get a suitable arrangement in car of sale save parts. Make beyond any doubt you to take photographs of your car from many edges so the potential purchasers can see its essential highlights.

Presently you realize how to make money selling on Amazon thus gather your items, open an account on Amazon and afterward begin posting them. Whatever you sell, guarantee you give the real condition of the products with the goal that you don't demolish your notoriety in the market.

Tips and Best Advice Resources For eBay and Amazon Resellers

You're starting at now trading on eBay and furthermore Amazon you will be especially familiar with a considerable amount of this information. To find where to get the most authoritative guide on the web. You're merely moving on eBay; you could be missing over 50% of your potential sales.

There are countless holding up at Amazon. Why not abuse the most shopped site on the web? Despite whether your business is eBay, Amazon or both, there are some broad guidelines to concentrate on. The achievement of your business will depend unimaginably on:

having the right instruments to find them in every practical sense endless wellsprings of useful stock robotizing the entire method shipping your stock in mass at exceptionally practical expenses explicitly to Amazon's warehouse esteeming your stock higher than your resistance while so far outperforming them keeping up your business from wherever.

Some Simple Guidelines and Tips:

1. Stamp yourself, your reputation is essential

2. Consider enduring PayPal portions

3. Grateful correspondence with your customers

4. Find your rebate procedure

5. Clear depiction of your product including shading photo

6. Provide associations with product tributes or surveys

7. Craigslist advancement for stock

8. Understand your customer

9. Review FBA Programs

10.Find trustworthy drop shipping association

11. Make sense of how to robotize your business

12. Use both eBay and Amazon to move your products
For your information: According to Amazon.com in a continuous survey of FBA sellers (those using FBA to pick, pack and ship their solicitations to buyers) they unveiled to Amazon the going with: 92% of survey respondents who have sent no short of what one unit through FBA uncovered their unit sales have extended since joining, 78% of survey respondents saw a typical augmentation in unit sales of 20 percent or more 89% of survey respondents would recommend FBA to a friend or partner.

Making Money Selling on Amazon

Utilizing the Internet as a way to make money is winding up considerably more typical. There are a few unique sorts of destinations that can return a profit for those wishing to make online sales. Making money selling on Amazon can be simple by following only a couple of straightforward insights.

The seller should initially make an online Amazon store. Setting up an account is free, and people can have a few distinct items like old magazines, books, and DVDs. These things must be in good condition to make a fruitful sale on Amazon. The seller can set their favored prices, rather than seeking after the best profits on a bartering.

It is important to have particular requirements when running an Amazon store on the web. Purchasers can rate their involvement with the seller, and a terrible rating will return less profit. Always speak the truth about the condition of the products, because nobody likes not getting what they think they paid for. There are sure classified decisions accessible to list under the condition. Make beyond any doubt to peruse all stipulations for each state to guarantee that the choice is exact. When shipping, always wrap sensitive items appropriately, so they don't appear harmed.

If conceivable, attempt to utilize without a doubt the most reduced prices, or if nothing else contrast and different prices on Amazon and go a little lower than the normal. This technique is best for people merely hoping to make some additional money as an afterthought while they wipe out their home, as opposed to attempting to return a noteworthy profit. By undermining different merchants, you will more than make up the profit edge by doing volume.

FIND THE TOP WAYS TO MAKE MONEY ON AMAZON

Throughout the years, Amazon has built up itself as a much online company and is frequently a popular decision for people hoping to make money online. In contrast to most different platforms, it offers you various ways to earn either as a seller, marketer or distributor. The company likewise gets great stamps for brilliant client benefit. Here's a gander at the different ways you can make money on Amazon.

1. Sell Products

The most popular and generally utilized technique to earn money on the website is selling products, for example, books, hardware, clothing things, and different merchandise. The beneficial thing is that it's simple and brings in real money genuine brisk. Fundamentally distinguish stuff you don't need and need to dispose of, show their condition and incorporate all the fundamental data. In case you're making new products, the strategy is the equivalent. You can even form an eCommerce website utilizing devices made accessible by Amazon.

2. Turn into An Affiliate

Another favorite way to make money on Amazon is to join the affiliate program. All things considered, how would you earn through this technique? You set up a link on your website or else send an email link, and after that get paid whenever somebody purchases a product through the loop. You can earn as much as 10% on every deal made through your website. Thus, if you have some great movement, you ought to think about turning into an affiliate.

3. Distribute Books

Arouse is no uncertainty a noteworthy accomplishment for Amazon and numerous people have (and proceed) made money by sharing their musings and information. If you have the energy for composing and have something you feel would be helpful to people, basically join to end up a Kindle Direct Publisher, at that point have the capacity to distribute for nothing and sell your work to a great many people who utilize the Kindle Store.

4. Promote

Pondering whether it's conceivable to make money on Amazon by advertising your things? It's understandable and straightforward to do as such. All you need is to set up promotions that will drive purchasers to your site, and in this manner increment your income. While picking the products to promote, attempt to go for those that are popular as well as liable to intrigue clients.

HOW TO MAKE $10,000 EVERY MONTH WITH AMAZON FBA

The model works by Amazon giving clients the capacity to send their products to its distribution centers, and having them "satisfied" by the hold monster (it sends them out) upon effectives buying.

The motivation behind why Amazon would do somewhat to get free specialty products which are both unique and profitable (you possess the products - they transport them for you), and halfway to make utilization of their enormous foundation (which they would pay for anyway).

It likewise add to their offering as a business, as it gives them considerably more different exhibit of products to add to their portfolio (which is practically their center upper hand).

The essential exciting point about the "FBA" model is that it is demonstrative of the new "computerized" business cultures that appears to have turned out to be considerably more common after the 2008 accident. Instead of keeping a lot of stock, overheads and active group organizations have taken to the Internet and web-based life to discover purchasers and makes leans ventures.

Gone the days when merchants decided the destiny of

products. Presently, new businesses, business visionaries, and ordinary people can make $10,000+ every month pay streams without owning any land. All the foundation, marketing, and satisfaction are taken care of by a free company (Amazon) - to which you only take every necessary step of sourcing a fruitful product.

Decide whether you don't get a kick out of the chance to pick up the favorable position from this technique for the venture, this instructionals exercises to clarify the way towards using Amazon FBA. As oppose to attempting to get by on scraps from a nearby market, the new "advanced" domains with all its guarantee is outstanding amongst other ways to gets your foot in the entryway of the news universe of big business.

How It Works

All businesses work similarly - purchase/manufacture a product, offer the product to a market, and any "profit" you're ready to make can either be utilized to live off or reinvest into more/better products.

The problem for a great many people is two-crease:

1)   They have no product

2)   They have no access to a market.

Whilst both are real problems - which would have

been a huge downside in a periods without the "advanced" medium - times have proceed onward to the indicate that boundaries section are low to the point that you just genuinely need to have the capacity to contribute a few $1,000 to have the opportunity of selling to a worldwide gathering of people.

Furthermore, regardless of the way that the "Amazon" opportunity has existed for just about ten years now (anybody can list products in its marketplace), the "FBA" model (which is uninvolved) has just begun to end up famous in the previous two years or somewhere in the vicinity.

You turned out poorly business school, to quickly disclose how to run a "fruitful" business, you fundamentally need to be capable give a product/administration to an extensive gathering of people. You'd typically go for around 30% net profit edge (after COGS and publicizing costs). How you do this is dependents upon you - the key is to purchase low, move high.

Presently, because the "advanced" domain is huge doesn't mean it's without the way in which "markets" ordinarily work. The rivalry is a unique power, similar to the possibility that since something is "simple," it very well may be reproduced moderately primarily by others (prompting a disintegration of your profits).

Selling on Amazon commonly works by giving access

to products which people either don't approach locally, or can acquire locally yet with significant limitations, (for example, shading/estimate issues), or with problems inconsistent quality of supply. As such, while the Amazon marketplace is tremendous - don't figure you can outsmart supply/request.

The excellent trick with "advanced" businesses is to give access to unique products (regularly made without anyone else or your company) which are just accessible through you. These products must be centered around answering that a great many people have no clue about, and accordingly suggests getting it through the Internet genuine.

Making a "unique" product is 1,000x less demanding said-than-done - the trick with it is to work on answers for your very own problems. Work toward honing a range of abilities, which you ready to apply to a extensive groups of onlooker, from which you'll have the capacity to recognize "products" which can be made and offered as a way to disentangle/take care of problems you've encountered yourself.

Begin Selling the hardest part, which is clarified underneath.

Selling The Products

The last step is to get the products sold. This is the hardest as you're for the most part at the impulse of the markets (both Amazon's and some other markets you may convey to the stage).

The trick to getting products purchased from Amazon is successful marketing.

Marketing boils down to a few points - the most outstanding being that you need to have the capacity to right-off the bat pull in consideration of potential purchasers and after that construct request - allowing them the chance to purchase your product as a way to fulfill that request.

These are the many ways to do this, you should recollect that in case you will do it adequately, you need to have the capacity to go out and market the product freely of whether it will be prevalent on Amazon. The less you need Amazon, the more probable it will be that you'll get people purchasing through the channel.

At long last, we should likewise bring up that any business you influence must to not be considered pure profit.

Your profit ONLY comes after your different costs have been accounted for, (for example, the genuine products themselves, boxes and marketing). It is a new kid on the block error to imagine that the cash you get from Amazon will be your "bring home" profit - it's not.

3 WAYS TO SELL PHYSICAL PRODUCTS USE FULFILLMENT BY AMAZON (FBA)

Did you realize that Amazon isn't the sellers of everythings on Amazon? Did you know ordinary people like you can sell physical products on Amazon? This open door has around for some time, yet it is ending up exceptionally famous right now because of instructive courses that are springing up all over.

The three ways you can sell physical product on Amazons: sell other people's products on Amazon and ships the orders yourself; sell other people's products on Amazon and let Amazon ship and sell your very own products on Amazon and let Amazon send them. The primary way is called trader satisfied. You list your stock on Amazon's site; however you fill or ship the orders yourself. The last two methods are called FBA.

Vendor satisfied might be the most straightforward way and minimum expensive to begin; however it is significantly more work. You list your products on Amazon's site. At the point when the products are gotten you are in charge of really shipping the products to the buyer. You can even sell things that you have around the house utilizing this strategy.

You can likewise use FBA to sell other people's products. For this situation, you go to the store and discover things that are as of now selling on Amazon, buy them, put your very own one of a kind UPC mark on the product, pack it, make the listing, ship it to an Amazon warehouse and sit tight for the buyer. There are advanced mobile phone applications that you can use to check products before you get them to enable you to decide whether you can make a benefit. You get a kick out of the opportunity to shop, are good at discovering deals and can ship a crate, at that point this might be the business for you. The other extraordinary thing about utilizing FBA is that your products are qualified for the Amazon Prime program. People who take part in this can get free multi-day shipping. Numerous people will pay somewhat more for a product for this comfort.

The second way to use the FBA program is to sell your products. You discover a product that you can sell, locate a private mark producer, make your image and sell your product. This is the most worthwhile of the ways to sell on Amazon; in any case, it requires more capital in advance. Additionally, it is more unsafe because you need to order stock.

As should be obvious selling on Amazon is unquestionably something that you can do to gain additional pay or turn into your full-time business. If you are hoping to begin an online store or you need to add an extra salary stream to your current online store, then you should consider FBA.

CHAPTER THREE

FULFILLMENT BY AMAZON - AND HOW IT CAN INCREASE YOUR SALES AND PROFITS BY 20% AND THAT'S ONLY THE TIP OF THE ICEBERG

Satisfaction by Amazon has prompted some astounding accounts of little endeavors all of a sudden encountering huge development in sales, some by having Amazon satisfy orders for goods typically processed directly to buyers by individuals selling on Amazon and sometimes by sellers on different locales, for example, eBay and Etsy, moving over to FBA.

A substantial number of sellers report a lot higher sales where buyers trust they are buying from a sizeable, dependable organization as opposed to from little and one individual endeavor. Purchasing directly through FBA builds buyer trust in the providing organization and improves the general probability of making a sale.

There are different advantages for sellers, one of the greatest being that FBA gives sellers a chance to leave the whole assignments of advancing items and managing buyers and satisfying requests to Amazon, while the seller centers around more profitable undertakings, such as sourcing new things, for

64

instance, and set up themselves in extra option marketplaces.

Furthermore:

- Product proprietors can remove occasions and time from works without reducing their selling exercises or tell potential buyers their conveyances may be postponed until the seller's arrival. Utilizing FBA, sellers can remove as long as they wish from business, as long as enough stock stays in Amazon's stockrooms to process orders.

- Some individuals hate managing direct with buyers and possibly going up against troublesome clients and enduring high feelings of anxiety. Utilizing FBA, it's Amazon that bargains with buyers and enquirers and handles all interchanges and all issues.

- FBA is amazingly easy to learn and put without hesitation quick, and bunches of data and downloadable pdf reports are accessible from Amazon to help speed the process of beginning up, finding out about FBA, submitting items and making sales. What are anticipating a massive installment from Amazon toward the finish of every month?

In any case, that is only a tad bit of what you have to know to achieve this conceivably unfathomably profitable business called Fulfillment by Amazon. In any case, it's sufficient to make you quick to begin another pay stream immediately. You won't be sad you did.

WHAT TYPE OF PRODUCTS WILL INCREASE YOUR PROFITS IN FBA - FULFILLMENT BY AMAZON

Sellers send their goods to Amazon and Amazon records them at the site, takes payment, manages enquirers and buyers, and satisfies orders. Before long a while later, Amazon sends a part of the returns back to sellers.

The process is straightforward and all around reported in basic well-ordered configuration at the site, however utilizing FBA can win sellers fundamentally not precisely doing all their very own selling and conveying goods direct to buyers.

Amazon's FBA charges are very high, not just for space to store sellers' goods in the organization's warehouses, yet additionally to pick goods from storage, and moreover pressing and conveying products to buyers.

For a low-profit product, it's conceivable Amazon could procure a more significant amount of the cost paid by buyers than sellers get from the organization. There are even accounts of sellers being out of pocket for sales made utilizing Fulfillment by Amazon.

Fortunately, various tips will enable you to profit on each sale.

For example,

- Choose products comparable however not equivalent to goods as of now drawing in high profit, standard sales at Amazon. When you find them, make your offer diverse to those different sellers, by offering a reward bundle with each purchase or including your eye-discovering bundling to private mark products to make them emerge from contending products. Give your products their very own one of a kind title and that way they can't be looked at or cost kept an eye on Amazon.

- Choose products coordinating high recurrence scan terms for different things at Amazon. Record catchphrases usual to Amazon's bestselling products like those you propose selling. Perceive what number of best-selling items contain at least one of those catchphrases and use the more regular precedents in your Amazon titles and listings. Use most usual watchwords for the sake of your product however without rupturing trademark laws or utilizing brand names.

- Choose little, lightweight things, because Amazon charges by space required to stock your products and by the heaviness of each bundle expelled from storage and bundled for conveyance.

To wrap things up, you will find FBA more costly than

doing everything yourself, except you will spare time spent on unproductive assignments and have the capacity to concentrate on more profitable errands, such as sourcing new products and extending your bestselling products to other showcasing scenes.

FULFILLMENT BY AMAZON AND HOW IT HELPS EXPLODE YOUR BUSINESS PROFITS

The vast majority acquainted with promoting on the web realize that as of now, however not every person comprehends what Fulfillment by Amazon includes.

Here are a few pointers:

- Sellers set up their goods as per rules set by Amazon, for example, by giving titles and depictions to their products and giving every product a reference name to enable Amazon to find it among a vast number of different goods in their immense warehouses. Sellers additionally demonstrate how and when their rights will touch base in one of those warehouses and which bearer will convey them.

- When goods land at one of Amazon's warehouses, it is set in stock and space took up by their products will charge the seller.

- Amazon will list the product on their site and sellers can drive their very own activity to those listings or abandon everything to Amazon.

- When something moves, Amazon picks and packs the product, takes payment, and conveys orders to buyers.

- Amazon at that point handles after sales questions and inquiries and managing objections and solicitations for the discount.

- Sellers are consistently refreshed on which of their products have sold and what amount has been earned.

Amazon has a useful pdf record pressed with necessary data for FBA sellers and heaps of product sourcing and selling tips accessible at their site. Find everything by tapping on 'Fulfillment by Amazon' base of any page at their website.

Presently you know how it functions, it's time to try the majority of that data, beginning today. That interface you have quite recently clicked is the place to start.

Selling Your Product With Fulfillment by Amazon

You have a product you are selling that you might want to have the capacity to ship to people around the nation who might want to order it, a simple method to gets your product set up to be shipped through Fulfillment by Amazon or FBA. People can order your products from its Amazon listing on the web, and Amazon will process and ship orders for you.

Why Use Fulfillment by Amazon?

Selling your product with Fulfillment by Amazon is a

lot simpler than shipping it yourself, for various good reasons. Amazon will as of now have the product in one of their fulfillment focuses, which implies you don't need to go to the mail station and hold up in line to mail bundles to people each time somebody orders from you. Amazon processes a considerable number of requests every day, so processing and shipping are simple for them.

You don't need to stress over people coming to you with product issues on the off chance that you ship your product with Amazon because Amazon handles all customer benefit and will assume liability for shipping issues. They will acknowledge returns and send out another product whenever asked.

People ought to be content with their shipping background because they will get free shipping on orders over $35.00. Amazon Prime individuals get free two-day shipping. You can rest guaranteed that your customers are in the best hands when their requests are satisfied through Amazon, who will ensure that they get their product in a timely way and good condition.

The best part is that utilizing Fulfillment by Amazon will expand your sales because Amazon is so natural to use and it is so natural for customers to share product listings.

CHAPTER FOUR

PRIVATE LABEL RIGHT - WHAT CAN YOU DO WITH FREE PRIVATE LABEL RIGHTS?

If you are in any capacity engaged with web advertising, you will know about the torrential slide of contributions of what are called 'Private Label Products' on the Internet today.

When you have free private label rights products, there are numerous ways that it can profit your business and help you make money. Various individuals utilize free private label rights in a wide range of styles. You need to build beyond any doubt that the private label rights that you will use for your business are justified, despite all the trouble. You would prefer not to give away something or move something, it is garbage. Doing this will hurt your business notoriety. So the principals thing you have to do is to make beyond any doubt it is well worth giving away.

Presently there are a few thing that you can do with free private label rights to encourage your business. Above all else, you can separate it into individual reports and place it into an automated assistant with the goal that you will have your mailing list that you can begin gathering names and email addresses for. This will always be a standout amongst the most critical tools you can have for your business. So you certainly need to consider doing this since it will help your company for quite a while into what's to come.

Next, you can likewise take the private label rights and change them any way that you need to. You can put your name on them and be the dealer and proprietor to a powerful business building tool. You can give this away on a pick on the page to enable you to get supporters for your mailing list.

Something else you can give away the free private label rights to other individuals. This will enable you to fabricate business contacts and discover customers that you can pitch different products to. At long last, you can even take more than one free private label rights products and set up them together into an eBook. This will give you the eBook product that you can give away or move. There are such a significant number of ways that you can utilize private label rights products to assist you with your business. You only need to use your brains to think of all the distinctive ways that you can enable your business to develop and make money with the utilization of free private label rights products. You can likewise do some research to make sense of this. The one realized actuality is that if you are not utilizing plr products in your business then you are passing up a powerful business tool that can enable you to make good money. Rundown: There are such a large numbers of things that you can do with free private label rights that will allow you to fabricate your business and make money. The individual label rights products can be a powerful business tool for you. Discover how you can utilize these sorts of products.

Private Label Product Optimization Against Consumer Packaged Goods

Did you realize that private labels products presently represent up to 45% of all retail sales in key European nations, and 21.5% of all retail sales in the U.S.? If you took a gander at these measurements ten or twenty years back, it would be an alternate story. Be that as it may, recently, private-label products have turned out to be progressively prevalent with consumers. However, you don't see these products burning through a large number of dollars on TV and print publicizing. Much of the time, private label products convey fundamentally higher edges to the retailer than the typical consumer delivered goods (CPG) brands.

Along these lines, it is astonishing that the private-label procedures are not sought after with the same dimension of energy or venture from their branded brethren. Is it since retailers are still entirely sold that the best way to spend their marketing spending plans is on customary promoting?

In recent years, most retailers have possessed the capacity to evacuate the disgrace so since quite a while ago attached to private-label products - that they are a substandard, "non-exclusive" option in contrast to the CPG brands. The reasons why consumers incline toward a specific branded product versus a particular private label product or the other way around are not promptly unmistakable.

In the staple business, research demonstrates that consumers show a significant bias for a branded product with specific sustenances and are more open to private label utilization with different nourishment. For instance, consumers are bound to buy an unmistakable brand name jar of beans; in any case, with regards to cheddar, they incline toward private label product. Maybe this is the reason the private label system isn't as widely acknowledged as CPG.

In any case, it can't be denied that retailers have a lot to pick up by at any rate trying things out with private label. Market research agencies can work with an extensive national retailer to enhance their private-label product technique and bundle plan. These agencies utilize the equivalent thorough branding advancement rehearses being used by the large CPG brands. This incorporates vivid investigations into the lives of consumers - how specific brands and products fit into their day by day lives. Market research agencies can figure out shouldn't something be said about a private label product addresses a consumer and pushes them to make the buy.

Many brand marketing agencies create idea testing projects to assess the different structure and informing alternatives. Some even have consumers evaluate the competitive products, both CPG and private label. In the end, the consumer needs to pick the private-label merchandise notwithstanding when it is shown right beside the natural brand symbol. Although the choice to purchase is made in the store, it is affected by more prominent CPG brands sometime before the consumer stops his or her vehicle.

Private Label Products - What You Need to Know to Use Them Properly

A private label products is one, after you buy it, gives the rights for you to rebrand it, change it and renovate it to wind up your own. So far as any other individual knows, you turn into the author and maker - the first author defers any copyright.

You should check the terms of any private label product permit since they do shift in what they let you do, yet by and large, products that give you individual label rights, or PLR, can be marked as your own. Furthermore, in this lies the issue.

Everybody who buys says, a specific private label

ebook, embeds their name as author, without making some other changes, there's probably going to be an entire cluster of a similar product on the web, with various people claiming to be authors. It would resemble a wide range of people all claiming to have composed. No one would realize who indeed wrote it, yet everyone is claiming to be the author would be under a cloud.

Private label products are in reality an essential venture on the off chance that you are hoping to create your very own product, yet you do need to do some work yourself, as opposed to merely changing the author's name to your own.

Here are a few rules to how you can make any private label product uniquely yours.

(1)   Private label products regularly accompany a word or other text document that you can edit. In this way, you can change the content in any way you need. Investing a little energy perusing the text and changing it to suit your style and thoughts, will make the product extraordinarily yours.

(2)   They say you shouldn't pass judgment superficially, yet not so with private label products. The cover of an ebook, for instance, is exceptionally unmistakable, and, except if you edit the realistic covers you generally get with PLR bargains, there are probably going to be a lot of a similar book showing

up under a lot of various names. You ought to considerably change the cover of a PLR book with the goal that your form is unique among the group.

(3)   With private label articles and the tremendous notoriety of Adsense, such a large number of people have fundamentally reordered their PLR articles onto a site, put it with Google AdSense squares, and distributed on the web. To such an extents, that numerous people are getting what's called the 'Google Slap' and having their records evacuated. Google detests copy content and will strike you on the off chance that you reorder PLR articles. You have to edit each article to make it uniquely extraordinary. Indeed, there's no such thing as a free lunch, particularly with private label products.

(4)   With private label ebooks, another strategy for making them your very own product is to cut them up into individual sections and utilize these in an autoresponder preparing arrangement for your bulletin supporters. Then again, you could likewise assemble some private label articles on a related subject and edit them together to make your very own unique ebook. Just create your very own cover, deals page, and so forth, and you have another product of your own to put to the markets.

(5)   There are instances of private label software and even private label videos; however these all have similar prerequisites. You have to change them, edit

them, add to them and adjust them with the goal that they are unique, on the off chance that you need to get the best an incentive from them. With privates label videos, it could be as necessary as including some text underneath, or your very own portion standard promotions. With private label software, a few arrangements are offering the source code, which implies, you are qualified, you can edit the system to make an entirely new product of your own. Or then again, you could re-appropriate this, and have a specialist delete it for you.

(6)   Perhaps a final private label product can be created from open area material which has lost its copyright security. You can utilize this content to bundle up a crisp book (it's what many present bookstores do), offering credit to the first author, yet adding text such that it was assembled and edited by you.

There are relatively perpetual approaches to tweak private label products; however the key is, you should dependably change them generously on the off chance that you are to have the capacity to get the best an incentive out of moving what ought to end up your unique product.

Thus, don't be tricked by the duplicate journalists out there who guarantee you a fortune utilizing private label products. There is dependably a catch and, with individual label products, the score is that additional work will be required on your part to legitimately redo any PLR product if you need to showcase it on the web effectively.

ADVANTAGES OF PRIVATE LABEL PRODUCTS

Private label products or administrations are those made or given by one company to offer under another company's brand. These are otherwise called store brands, private brands, or private goods. Individual brands are accessible in a wide range of ventures from nourishment to beautifying agents. Previously, these products were frequently viewed as lower cost choices to real brands, yet numerous private brands are presently displayed as premium brands and contend with existing name brands.

There are numerous favorable circumstances for retailers to advance private label products. The bundling and labels can be uniquely custom fitted to meet particulars, including product name, portrayal, company's logo, and contact data. Private labeling permits more authority overestimating methodologies. There is additionally more opportunity for retailers to make their marketing designs and to control their very own stock in stocks. With higher edges conceivable, there is a prominent open door for the benefit. Private branding enables retailers to make a customized and unique picture, which advances more grounded customer dependability.

Private labeling takes into consideration more noteworthy authority over numerous elements - including sales, marketing, and circulation. Retailers can have finish authority over product dissemination with individual label product. The products are accessible from the retailer - customers won't go into a mainstream megastore and locate the own brand product at a lower cost. Customers won't find the private brand product elsewhere on the web either.

With private labeling, retailers can secure products that are as of now created, or that can be changed and re-branded in an individual mold. Essentially, retailers can control numerous business perspectives, and make their unique product. They can customize the products, include their data, extra materials, logos, titles, and so forth. This should all be possibles in significantly less times than it would take to build up the product starting with no outside help.

In recent years there has been a critical increment in the number of private label brands. This is especially valid in Europe, where privates label goods represent a large portion of the products sold in supermarkets. This figure is nearer to 25% in the United States, yet the pattern gives off an impression of being expanding.

Private brands originate from a few unique source. Various organization currently offer contract fabricating for private goods. Vast national brand producers regularly supply private label brands. Sporadically, contending a similar enormous producer even makes brands. Fixings, quality, and structures frequently contrast a considerable amount among these products, be that as it may.

Private brand goods are additionally procured from little, quality makers that spend significant time specifically product lines. Regularly, these organizations focus on delivering private label brands only. There are likewise territorial brand makers that create individual label products for specific markets.

Private label brands are accessible in a wide range of ventures from sustenance to beautifying agents. These brands help make a unique product and customize a brand for retailers. Retailers with solid private label brands make excellent sales open doors for themselves. They can manufacture esteem and acknowledgment from the customers. Private brand products enable retailers to separate their products from rivals' products and give consumers an option in contrast to different brands.

PROFITABLE PRODUCTS TO SELL ON AMAZON

The watchword is profit - moderately easy to "sell" products (directly sell smartphones or innovation products), yet your profit edges will be revolting.

What a great many people don't understands is that the money you "gather" from business merely is part of the story.

"Full" retail buys provide a gross salary. To decide the profit, you need to limit COGS (Cost of Goods Sold) and any additional "regulatory" costs, for example, advertising, warehousing, and staffing costs.

While the charm of the "computerized" domain has urged millions to raid into its profundities, it isn't exceptional. Regardless you need to represent profit (primary concern) as opposed to by and large gross (top line) to keep up your logical soundness (and suitability).

The "online" business world nearly reflects its disconnected partner, which implies that in case you're hoping to exploit the plenty of changes made with any semblance of Amazon, YouTube, and so on - you'll need to take a gander at how they function... as "markets."

YouTube is a market for stimulation, Twitter is a

market for consideration and Amazon is a market at item costs. Understanding this places you in the excellent position of having the capacity to decide a more compelling way to provide solutions to members in said markets.

Supply/Demand.

The most important thing to value that it's about supply and demand - the foundation of a "free market."

Supply/Demand expresses that if there is demand, supply will doubtlessly pursue. Over-supply brings "prices" down. Under-supply brings "prices" up.

The most important thing to consider is the manner by which demand is made/affected.

Demand is the foundation of whether a "product" will sell, and is the reason any semblance of "innovation" products always do well online (because people need to guarantee they're getting the most recent and most noteworthy parts).

In this manner, while thinking about what to "sell" on Amazon, you're fundamentally taking a gander at which products have demand and are under-provided. High prices may not show the supply circumstance, but rather people will by, and large either keep down on "superfluous" buy, or request varieties of provided solutions.

The critical thing to considers is that a great many people are centered around "supply" (normally over-supply, for example, you'd see from products which either have a ton of purchasers or a ton of merchants ("smartphones" being a prime precedent).

By selling a "me-as well" product, you may get deals however you'll constantly have no profit. "Tech" space, profits are negligible because the volume is so high. Balance this with any semblance of furniture where volume is moderately low; profits can be a lot higher.

The facts of the matter is that the "price" you accomplish on any of the advanced platforms is vigorously reliant on the quality and integrity of the solution, as opposed to whether different organizations are now offering it.

To this end, coming up next are a portion of the more compelling solutions/products to sell through Amazon:

Embellishments For Popular Products

This works particularly well for smartphones, PCs and video supports/amusements. If you locate a favorite product (mainly entertainment), you ought to have the capacity to source complimentary embellishments for it.

Shoddy To-Make Kickstarter Products

Kickstarter (swarm subsidizing platform) is a goldmine for the curious Amazon retailer. In addition to the fact that you have SPECIFIC postings of products which have been supported (and the genuine information to help them), however, you have a diagram for products that a market will need. Probably the best classes for this are in the "imaginative" space - books and table games. Presently, the caution here is to NOT rip-off the products being referred to - utilize them as a point of perception of what you could purchase/motivate made to complement the demand they have PROVEN to exist.

Boxed VIRTUAL Products

You can get STEAM codes modest, why not pay some money to get them boxed? Shouldn't something be said about on the off chance that you discovered a few "guides" doing admirably on ClickBank's marketplace (there are a TON of amusement guides for any semblance of World of Warcraft Gold and so on there)? An incredible trap is to locate a virtual product that is now selling and merely make a physical duplicate. You CANNOT rip-off the other product. If you don't have anything of your own to include, only purchase their book and change it or something. The fact is that you need to provide a one of a kind offer to another market - with demand ALREADY demonstrated.

Custom/Unique Products You Have Access To LOCALLY

One of the BIGGEST oversights new sellers make with Amazon is fundamentally simply doing precisely equivalent to every other person. They'll even utilize the equivalent "source" in China (using Alibaba obviously). The best people can fundamentally "source" their very own products locally (or maybe from their providers) and after that offer them as equivalent products on the Amazon platform. For instance, you may know a neighborhood clothing provider who'll sell you shabby garments (discount) - you'd have the capacity to put them onto Amazon while focusing on useful clothes that are on the platform as of now.

What Products To Sell - 10 Ways To Know What People Want

What products to offer to make money fast? You need to make money quickly you need to realize what people need and what issue they have. Along these lines, you will recognize what products to move, and you will give them an appropriate arrangement.

Ten ways to recognize what people need to perceive what products to pitch them to acquire money on the web.

1. Search on ClickBank's Marketplace

Complete a search at on ClickBank's marketplace and take a gander at first 5-7 products of your market. Search for various classes in the ClickBank's marketplace for those products that are related to your picked market.

2. Research your market-related discussions

Since there are gatherings for pretty much every market, pick the ones of your territory and make research: search for the most talked about topics, for what are people's issues, wants, concerns and needs. At that point think to answer them.

3. Discover blockbuster books at Amazon

Blockbusters books are products that move the most. You take a gander at Amazon - segment Books - and search for watchwords or expressions that are related to your market, you will discover (go to Advanced Search) an incredible list of books positioned by the top of the line.

4. Research Yahoo Answers on classifications

Research that classification that is related to your market at Yahoo Answers. Search for what are peoples needs, issues, and objectives. You will discover a ton of thoughts.

5. Make a study from your blog or website

You can find what people need on the off chance that you make a review on your blog or website. Get some information about topics related to your market.

6. Look in popular article directories

Go to most popular article directories like EzineArticles, GoArticles or Isnare and look of the most seen articles that are related to your market.

7. Search the most popular blogs

Search the most popular blogs related to your market.

8. Solicit supporters from your mailing list

Solicit supporters from your mailing list what topics intrigue them the most. At that point get the most needed topic.

9. Broaden your research on disconnected magazine, newspapers, and books

Go to your neighborhood library, bookstore or news-stand and research on magazine, newspapers, and books to perceive what are the most needed topics related to your market.

You can utilize INFOTRAC framework from your library to see late issues of newspapers and magazines. Or on the other hand approach the bookkeeper for "Books in Print" reference volume, that is a comprehensive catalog of books listed by title and subject.

When you have a list of magazine and newspapers that contain the essential articles, discover them and do research. Why magazine and newspapers? Since they are up and coming.

10. Check out your prompt condition and investigate TV adverts and projects

Figure out how to watch people, things and activities around your prompt condition. Listen to what people ask, search for and talk about.

The media have increasingly affected our lives, and it very well may be utilized as a magnificent way to create new thoughts. Checking the TV listings and breaking down what is on TV and current issues can assist you in finding what people need.

Step by step to Source Products to Sell on the Amazon Website

So you've understood that the Amazon website can be an extraordinary place to move goods on for a profit, however that doesn't answer the essential inquiry. How might you source products to run on Amazon? Where are those immeasurably vital goods to offer ongoing to originate from? Here are only a couple of places to consider, helping you to begin.

1. Your carport/storage room

You don't have to live in a house for long to begin to aggregate a collection of bits and sways that you don't generally require any longer. If you are searching for something to move why not start in your carport or upper room? Moving a portion of these odds and ends has a double advantage; it gets out the messiness in your own home, and it can get some extraordinary profit, which you would then be able to use to put toward new stock to move.

2. Your neighborhood philanthropy shop/vehicle boot deal

Other people are in the very same circumstance as you; they have loads of 'garbage' in their homes that they need to offer on to make a touch of money. Keep in mind forget that one man's garbage is another man's gold, and philanthropy shops or vehicle boot deals can be incredible places to source products to move on Amazon. Simply make beyond any doubt you have thought of the amount you can remain to make from each buy; you would prefer not to spend a considerable measure of money to understand that you can't make any profit moving the things on the web.

3. Your loved ones

Why not offer your internet pitching administrations to your loved ones? You could move on a portion of their unwanted goods, keeping a part of the profits for yourself and passing on the rest. Simply make beyond any doubt you are clear about the amount you're holding before beginning; you would prefer not to estrange your closest and dearest in the quest for a couple of pounds!

4. A distributor

A wide range of organization around the world can offer goods at a decreased, or a discount, price. A portion of these places may exist inside your very own town or city, while others can be found in various areas with a quick online search. Search for discount suppliers in your specialty market region to check whether they can offer you a few goods at a price that gives you a lot of profit when you go to move the things on.

5. eBay

The last alternative to consider is that of eBay or other online sale websites. Here and there it is conceivable to get your hands on a lot on these websites for goods that you can move on Amazon for a profit. In any case, won't those Amazon customers only go to eBay to get a similar deal? Not in the least! Numerous purchasers naturally go to buy from Amazon without ever notwithstanding checking the price; they accept that Amazon offers the best deal and, if not, it, at any rate, accompanies brilliant client benefit. You can exploit this by sourcing stock to move on Amazon on different websites where it might be fundamentally less expensive.

DIFFERENCES BETWEEN FULFILLMENT BY AMAZON AND SELLERS FULFILLED PRIME.

Any retailer extremely valuable will realize that a decent nearness on Amazon is indispensable to the accomplishment of their business – while permeability on Amazon Prime is much more vital. This is the reason getting to holds with the Fulfillment by Amazon (FBA), and Seller Fulfilled Prime (SFP) programs is urgent.

The retail goliath and their Prime programs, at last, assume a featuring job in the day-to-day tasks of online retailers of every kind imaginable. With 60 million Prime members overall spending a normal of $1,200 every year – contrasted with the $500 every year usual spent by non-members – Prime is a market you'd be insane not to take advantage of.

The two programs that permit you access to those brilliant Prime racks Fulfillment by Amazon and Seller Fulfilled Prime – otherwise called merchant fulfilled Prime.

Both offer one major component: they enable you to move on Amazon Prime, giving you an excellent introduction and opening your business to that massive market. That is about where the likenesses end. FBA and SFP are in a general sense altogether different and have highlights that primarily ensure they will speak to specific businesses relying upon size, productivity, and goals.

To enable you to figure out which program might be best for your business, I've laid out five critical differences between having your merchandise fulfilled by Amazon or through you, using their Seller Fulfill Prime programs;

1. Fulfillment.

The most striking differences between FBA and SFP is the manner in which your items are fulfilled.

As the name recommends, Fulfillment by Amazon means Amazon fulfills your inventory. They deal with everything. You send a segment of your list to Amazon's fulfillment focuses, where it's stored until the point that a customer chooses to get it. Amazon at that point picks, packs and ships the items to your customers, while you kick back and benefit.

With Seller Fulfilled Prime, fulfillment is in grasp. Customers will buy through Amazon Prime, of course; however your organization delivers the items accurately, with no mediation from Amazon. You utilize the Amazon Prime brand name and shipping rules, yet it's dependent upon you to pick, pack and ship to your customers.

So what's the trick with SFP?

Shipping! An enormous difference between having items fulfilled by Amazon and merchant performed is that the merchant needs to pay for shipping. This can destroy your edges and conceivably result in a negative deal in case you're not watchful.

Fees

"Kick back and benefit," "This is unrealistic," you thought – and if inadequately oversaw, you might be correct.

This is on account of FBA's fees. As an individual who has been a piece of the Fulfillment by Amazon program will know, Amazon's fulfillment fees can rapidly eat into your benefit. In all reasonableness to Amazon, they thoroughly take care of you, so you can anticipate that they will request something in return. Apparently, that includes some significant downfalls.

For instance, take one little non-media item fulfilled by Amazon. They can charge around $3-4 for order dealing with, picking and pressing, weight taking care of and storage. Despite what you're moving, these fees can heighten quick.

SFP clients, then again, can stay away from these fees — as you're not sending anything to Amazon to be stored, taken care of, pressed or returned, there is no purpose behind them to receipt you with eye-watering fees. It's more work, usually — in addition to you have your very own shipping costs to manage — yet that bit of edge is all yours.

Storage

The storage of your inventory is another zone that features the differences between these two Prime programs.

Fulfillment by Amazon is a convincing suggestion for retailers moving entirely on Amazon. For whatever is left of us, we move on however many deals channels as could be expected under the circumstances — why? Since multichannel customers are more beneficial! You could utilize Amazon's multichannel fulfillment administrations; however then you lose control of your valuable inventories.

To be a merchant fulfil Prime member you'll need your ware house. By keeping controls of your inventory and fulfillment, you'll need a ware house and ware house staff of your own which can be cost to get, keep up and team. Also, as a merchant fulfilled Prime member, you HAVE to transport Prime order same day. This mean your warehouse must be streamlined and process orders effectively.

Inventory Control

Inventory control positively ties in with the storage issues featured.

With Fulfillment by Amazon, after you've sent your inventory to Amazon's fulfillment ware houses, it's no more. This sounds like an undeniable proclamation; however, the effect of this means you can't only go down to the warehouse to see precisely what you have when you need to.

Like this, it tends to be somewhat dubious to decide precisely what's in stock, which can without much of a stretch lead to stale inventory. Over this, Amazon charges punishment fees for list stored in a Fulfillment Center for longer than a half year.

The difference with regards to SFP is that you have finish control over your stock — no part inventory between Amazon's warehouses and your own. All your list can be stored in one focal area, which means you have finish control over your stock. This is a major in addition to if you move on various deals channels and additionally have a physical area. This is considerably more obvious with regards to occasions, for example, Prime Day or Black Friday, as there's no restriction on the amount you can move.

Returns

At the point when Amazon fulfills your inventory, the brand will deal with returns for your sake, and also give their 'top-class' customer benefit. This is extremely helpful for little businesses who will profit by the time and assets this will spare.

SFP sees your organization handle all returns, which means you'll need your very own performances as well as customer benefit division. Notwithstanding, this brings its advantages because — while Amazon sends FBA members a full box of returned products — things are positively less obscure with SFP.

The in addition to the point with this is you can without much of a stretch distinguish which returned item connections to which order — bringing about more shot of keeping away from potential customer misrepresentation.

In any case, remember that Amazon's essential spotlight is on their customer encounter. They need the customer to have a similar shopping background paying little heed to what program the item was fulfilled through.

This is the reason, in mid-2017, Amazon declared another approach that caused agitation among numerous sellers on the SFP program. The progressions mean sellers who satisfy their very own orders will be liable to the same guidelines as those fulfilled by Amazon. One part of the new arrangement set up that all items would be 'consequently approved' for return – which means purchasers can return items to the seller at the seller's cost, without reaching the seller first.

Bounty to Consider

These five differences inevitably feature the primary varieties between Fulfillment by Amazon and the more current Seller Fulfilled Prime programs.

Both SFP and FBA have certain favorable circumstances and impediments, and they will speak to various businesses with various desires. What's more, it's additionally worth referencing the strict necessities retailers need to meet to be a piece of Amazon's merchant fulfilled Prime program.

Utilizing SFP, numerous sellers won't observe cost reserve funds – instead, they may see their fulfillment costs increment marginally. Be that as it may, the first advantage is in the capacity to move more at higher volumes over numerous channels – this is the thing that makes up for the costs while being an SFP member.

While it's not in every case simple to figure out which

program is best for your business – satisfying orders yourself or having them fulfilled by Amazon – remember that you are not the only one when it with regards to settling on this essential choice.

CHAPTER FIVE

THE BENEFITS OF ORDER FULFILLMENT SERVICES

Provide to customers in each of the pieces of business. From services to products, companies are there to address the issues of its customers and give them an excellent service that they'd be glad to utilize over and over. If you maintain a business that includes moving products, you'll realize that it is so essential to ensuring brilliant customer service, particularly on the off chance that you run your products globally. Ensuring that customers get their products flawless and promptly can once in a while be dubious, yet order satisfaction can make this procedure much smoother.

What is order satisfaction?

Order satisfaction alludes to the aggregate of the sales proceeds from the underlying sales request to the product being conveyed to the customer. Although the procedure sounds basic, it can include a few people and be more mind-boggling than you may understand. For instance, you were somebody that moves handcrafted products on the web, you would get a sales request through your webpage, which could be anything from an individual website to betterknownbetter-known eCommerce channels like Amazon and E-narrows.

When you've got the order to ask for, you have to ensure that the product is packaged up and sent to your customer's area inside the predefined period. In case you're only one individual working from your PC at home, this implies you'll need to ensure that your costs cover postage and packaging through Royal Mail or related conveyance services, and as a general rule you can wind up losing cash over the long haul.

Order satisfaction services give both individual sellers and organizations of all sizes the chance to cut a portion of those extra costs and guarantee that the majority of the products you move are put away, took care of and conveyed by a solid outsider surface. Making utilization of order satisfaction services from a fortified distribution center office is extraordinary compared to other approaches to maintain your business all the more effectively while setting aside some cash and keeping the customer fulfilled.

Where would I be discover these service?

There are a lot of capacity distribution centers out there that will stock your products until the point that the time seeks them to be delivered, and by and large, it's best to keep it nearby. Discover a stockroom with a scope of bed arrangements and order satisfaction services that can be utilized by associations and people with various necessities and prerequisites. There are distribution centers that offer flexible price packages that can be customized to meet your particular requirements as a seller.

For instance, there are distribution centers that give a 'pay as you go' service that implies you just need to pay for the 'pick and pack' services when you move something. This is perfect for the individual seller or the little business that can't manage the cost of a month to month fee for capacity and order satisfaction. There aren't any covered up or starting fees to stress over, and you can quit your agreement at whatever point you like. Regardless of whether you're a strong organization that needs assistance with handling orders or you're merely somebody that is moving things online from home, exploiting the incredible order satisfaction services accessible must be useful for business.

HOW TO ACCURATE CALCULATE YOUR AMAZON SELLER AND FBA FEES

Any individual who is thinking about moving their product on Amazon has to realize how to decide their gross profit margin. Numerous sellers who have raced to get their product online have made brisk counts to discover later that their product was making beside nothing. All that works for an 8% profit margin.

What's more, a standout amongst the most vital bits of overhead costs is the Amazon seller fees. Since Amazon is enabling you to get to their sales stage, they'll be taking a cut from each unit that you move. When you consider the activity numbers on Amazon, that is a reasonable arrangement.

Numerous sellers get confounded when they endeavor to deal with the majority of the substance Amazon offers on seller fees. To ensure you're figuring your overhead effectively, we will separate Amazon seller fees into simple advances. Before the finish of this book, you'll have the capacity to unquestionably decide your total profit margin by coordinating the majority of Amazon's fees.

1. Amazon Fees for Selling on Amazon

Amazon separates every one of their products into 38 classes (and one classification entitled "Everything Else"). Every one of these classes is taken care of distinctively by Amazon, making either a referral fees percentage of the product's sale price or a minimum referral fee (whichever fee is more).

So for instance, you sold a product in the kitchen classification for $20, you would be charged a 15% referral fees ($3) because 15% of $20 is more than the $1 minimum referral fee. Be that as it may, you sold a kitchen product for $3, you'd be charged a $1 minimum referral fees because the minimum referral fee is over 15% of $3 ($0.45).

The minimum referral fee isn't appropriate to all classes. A few classes require a referral percentage paying little respect to the sale price (i.e., Video Games and Consoles)

Ordinarily, except if your price point is around $5 or $6, Amazon will remove the referral percentage from your sales price.

2. Amazon Fees for Using Fulfillment by Amazon

Naturally, you could generally discover another drop shipper or ship the products yourself, yet re-appropriating your transportation to Amazon is an incredible method to free you up to focus on other greater undertakings in your business.

However, regardless of whether you utilize Amazon FBA or a drop shipper, there will be a fee included. The thing that matters is that Amazon will expel your FBA fee specifically from your sales and doesn't expect you to pay a different bill. At regular intervals, you'll be given your sales profit with delivery and Amazon seller fees effectively taken out.

Is your product a media items or a non-media items?

Media items incorporate books, music, videos, video games and consoles, DVDs, and programming and PC games. In case your the product isn't one of those items, it is a non-media item.

Is your product standard size or larger than average?

Your product gauges 20 lbs. Or on the other hand less, 18" or less on its longest sides, 14" or less on its median sides, and 8" or less on its most limited side, it will be viewed as standard size. Any product that surpasses those measurements will be viewed as Oversize.

For each product, there are three necessary fees related to utilizing FBA.

Order Handling ($0 for media/$1 p/unit for non-media)

Picks and Pack ($1.06 p/unit)

Weight Handling (reliant on weight and size)

Applying what we realized

So how about we place this into reality.

You're moving a kitchen product on Amazon for $20 and utilizing FBA.

To begin with, you have to decide your referral percentage fee. Taking a gander at the outline, you realize that Amazon deducts 15% from your sale price since you're moving on their stage.

Sale Price ($20) - Referral Percentage ($3 [15%]) = $17

Also, you have to decide if your product is media or non-media. Since your product is a kitchen utensil, you realize that it's non-media. In this way, you would already be able to recognize that both an order handling fee and a pick and pack fee will be connected.

$17 - Order Handling Fee ($1) - Pick and Pack Fee ($1.06) = $14.94

Also, finally, you'll have to decide the weight of your product. Suppose that because of its tallness, it is viewed as a vast standard size, and it gauges 1 lb. Utilizing the diagram above, we can ascertain the weight handling fee to be $0.96.

$14.94 - Weight Handling Fee ($0.96) = $13.98

Presently you have a real picture of what your total Amazon fees will be, and this number can be utilized to compute your overhead. Notwithstanding your product, you ought to dependably use this equation to ascertain your Amazon fees:

Amazon profit = Sale Price - Referral Percentage - Order Handling - Pick and Pack - Weight Handling

Before you ever dispatch your product, it's fundamental that you decide your total profit margin by deducting your COGS (cost of merchandise sold) and overhead expenses from your sale price. At that point would you be able to realize that your business has long-haul potential. A standout amongst the most fundamental of these overhead costs is your Amazon fees.

At whatever point you're first beginning your Amazon

business, the pages of data gave to figure your Amazon fees can be overpowering and confounding. Ideally, this book will enable you to stroll through this procedure somewhat more effortlessly. Utilize the recipe above, at that point begin deciding if your price point is sufficiently high or not.

Settling on cost successful choices is extraordinarily imperative to any web-based business. It's additionally essential to set aside extra cash where you can on showcasing, and an extraordinary method to do that is with Sales backed so you can get more product audits from your consistent customers without spending a considerable measure of additional cash on product advancements.

5 WAYS TO FIND BEST PRODUCTS TO SELL ON AMAZON

With the approach of the web during the '90s, E-commerce has spread like fierce blaze. Buyers have moved from customary shopping to web-based business.

Individuals have been referred to make as much as $5000 in an hour by selling on Amazon. This can be somewhat precarious. Remember that Amazon moves in excess of 300 million individual products. What's more, just by selling the correct products you can turn into a successful seller.

Here are five ways to locate the best products to move on Amazon.

1. Start by Discovering Profitable Products

You can locate the most profitable items to move on Amazon absent much understanding. Amazon gives all of you the essential data to understand market patterns and products that run.

You need to understand what makes an item profitable. Criteria like shipping weight, notoriety, category, and competition all assume an outstanding job here. You need to distinguish products that meet the vast majority of the criteria.

Research the Shippable and Sellable Factors

When searching for products you need to initially think about three things: Shipping cost, discount pricing, and Amazon Seller expenses.

Endeavor to buy products thinking about the accompanying specs:

The cost ought to be 25% to 35% of your target selling price

Your target selling price ought to be in the scope of $10 to $50.

The product(s) ought to be lightweight, i.e., around 2-3 lbs. counting box and bundling.

Essential and solid items that would reduce the danger of misfortune from harm.

Evergreen or ordinary utilize items, which means they can be utilized consistently.

Better quality products when contrasted and the competition.

2. Check For Competition

To get benefits, you need a product that is priced gainfully, found and sent effortlessly, and accessible.

The following are the key factors that determine whether your product(s) meets these criteria.

Products that are not at present being sold by real brands and Amazon sellers.

Comparable items that have Amazon's Best-Seller Rank (BSR) of 5000 or lower.

Items that can be sought under different product classifications and watchwords.

Driving product catchphrases having not more than 10,000 hunts/month.

Comparative product postings having under 50 reviews

3. Gain From Amazon Product Listings

In the product depiction, you will discover different data about the product, for example, product measurement, weight, and so on. From that point, you can determine if your product is an evergreen one.

Post for the accompanying criteria to locate the most sellable and profitable items:

Item pricing: The thing is priced at $29.99. The pricing is flawless as it falls under the pricing section of $10 to $50.

Product dimensions and weight: Here you can find that the product weighs 2.78 pounds and has a dimension of 6.5 x 4.5 x 3 inches. This size and weight will help in chopping down the shipping cost.

Generally, specs and deals are positioning: You will find that the Amazon BSR of this product is 3. This is way under the BSR 5000 position. Likewise, it very well may be found under the toys and recreations category effortlessly.

Client reviews: You will find that the product has more than 2000 reviews from purchasers. This is way past the 500+ reviews rank making it a very much confided in the product. This additionally shows the product has a considerable measure of interest in the market.

4. Discover What Others are Selling

Do you realize that little scale sellers are becoming wildly successful by selling specialty items? From carefully assembled pieces to customers and one of a kind gems items and even live bugs. Along these lines, they reduce the competition from huge sellers and from Amazon itself.

Amazon is excellent with regards to upselling products. It keeps a segment exhibiting prescribed products underneath a product's depiction. This urges purchasers to consider the products that are being exhibited.

Notice how Amazon recommends product matching with the previously mentioned smash hit. Here, proposed products may not be "bestsellers" themselves, but rather as a seller, you can determine what the products different sellers are selling are.

5. Select Your Source For Products

When you are finished looking into on which products to move, you should start contemplating sourcing them.

Here are two spots from where you can start your inquiry:

Alibaba: If you want to move on Amazon, Alibaba is a decent place to source your products. It is where you can source reasonable imports. Something to be thankful for about Alibaba is that it encourages you to find out about product sourcing. This is to a high degree accommodating if you are new to the business.

Discount marketplaces: Wholesale purchasers markets are another way of sourcing your products. Discount markets are arranged in each significant city in the US. Furthermore, the best part is, they center around each possible industry. To find your closest discount market google it. Likewise, keep in mind to include the product name or category you are keen on. The Dallas Market Center, NY NOW Wholesaler Gift and Home, Los Angeles Gift and Home and Las Vegas Market are significant discount markets in the US worth visiting.

There's nothing more regrettable than seeing your product marketing campaign flop before your eyes. This can be the aftereffect of your shoppers not needing the product to a noteworthy seller suffocating your business. The above focuses will enable you to understand the science behind deciding successful product deals.

Amazon represents almost 50% of every single online deal made in the US. Henceforth, there is a great deal of profitable open doors for sellers. The main thing that you should worry about is market research and concentrating on making a momentous purchasing background for your clients. You will need great reviews and individuals returning to you. It's not just about what number of products you can move multi-day. The good metric you should concentrate on is what number of rehash clients you can get. This will enable you to end up a successful seller on Amazon.

CHAPTER SIX

MANUAL FOR STARTING A
FULFILLMENT BY AMAZON BUSINESS

Business display keeps on developing in popularity, and all things considered. On a fundamental level, it's equivalent to a traditional e-commerce business. Be that as it may, rather than your satisfying orders one by one, Amazon store products for you and picks, packs and ships them out to customers.

This makes much simpler for you to construct your business without agonizing over the logistics of warehouses, bundling materials, dispatches, etc. With private labeling, you additionally have the chance to manufacture your brand and website, in this manner expanding the estimation of your business.

Raring to go? Here's our essential guide for beginning an FBA business.

The FBA business demonstrates it enables you to use Amazon's dynamic conveyance system and customers bases. As noted, Amazon will ware house your products, fulfill orders and even give customer benefit, so you don't need to be hands-on with each part of the business.

What this implies for business people is that you can act like a major enterprise without the cerebral pain of really being one. You can concentrate on finding product opportunities while Amazon handles the lay for your sake.

In an ordinary e-commerce business, you need to make sense of the logistics of sending products to your customers in a timely way. With FBA, Prime individuals get most orders transported to their entryway inside two to five days.

Another standard test with an e-commerce store is that reviewing and posting other products available to be purchased can increase the unpredictability of your business. With FBA, you should merely transport the products to Amazon's warehouse, and the organization will assume control from that point. You can undoubtedly increase your product determination without fundamentally adding to your remaining task at hand.

Make an Amazon seller account.

First of all: To get your FBA business ready for action, you will need to make an Amazon seller account. Go to Amazon's website, look down to the footer and search for the heading stamped "Profit with Us." Then, tap on the connection that peruses "Sell on Amazon."

Now, you can either join as an "Individuals" or a "Proficient." When you join as a "Singular," you won't be charged a month to month membership expense. If you're hoping to construct a business as time goes on, you'll need to join as a "Proficient." The first month is free, and from that point forward, it's $39.99 every month in addition to selling charges.

Other than that, the information exchange process is generally direct. Adhere to the onscreen guidelines and finish setup.

Reveal product opportunities and build up your private label.

There are various distinctive ways to use the FBA display, yet the most popular method is private labeling. The thought is to set up a brand or label, apply it to your product and sell it on Amazon.

In the first place, you should do your Amazon product research. This is an essential advance for an assortment of reasons. You enter an offensive product category and sell a product for more than your opposition selling it for you could loss money on that product. You set aside the opportunity to find a popular product category, do a competitive examination, think about product audits and recognize a product that you can enhance or sell at a superior value; you'll have discovered the sweet spot.

Another favorite way to sell products through Amazon is with the local exchange - purchasing a brand name products and flipping it on Amazon for the benefit. This is a lot simpler way of profiting on Amazon, at any rate temporarily.

With private labeling, you need capital. Ordering individual label products may cost you a few thousand dollars, yet on the off chance that you're hoping to assemble a benefit that can later be sold, this is the course you need to go in.

Another crucial bit of the riddle is your provider. You can't profit if you don't have products in stock, so you need to guarantee that the time delay between the situation and conveyance of the order is as short as it can be.

Tips for developing and scaling your FBA business

Seek after your energy. You appreciate doing it; you will stay with it for more. Find a product category that interests and energizes you.

Increase your product contributions. You should do legitimate research for each new product offering you make. Having more products can decrease the danger of your business getting to be reliant on only one outcome.

Enhance your Best Sellers Rank. BSR is a vital measurement for both your customers and your deals. This is additionally a key factor when the time comes to sell your business. Purchasers will need to see relentless development in your BSR rank after some time.

Fabricate your brand website. As you keep on extending your private label product contributions, you'll need to fabricate an expert, devoted site for your business. This gives you another way to advertise your products, and can likewise make your business alluring to potential purchasers.

Turn into an Amazon Associate. Increase your incomes by turning into an association with Amazon. Allude customers to your products from your very own site, and begin earning commissions.

Earning potential

What amount do FBA business proprietors acquire? What is the earning potentials of an FBA business?

Last contemplations

Albeit beginning an FBA business will require in advance capital, the exertion will be not even close as escalated as it would be with a traditional e-commerce business. Getting business off the ground is the simple part. Finding ways to become your FBA business is the more troublesome part. Exploit the assets accessible to you, and systematize your procedures as you go.

EASY STEPS TO MAKES MONEY ONLINE THROUGH AMAZON DROP SHIPPING

There are different ways and platforms to makes money online, one of them that grabbed omnipresence starting late is drop shipping through Amazon. Various individuals are making countless doing this business.

Drop shipping has its inclinations over the customary online stores where you have to stocks the goods in your store and ship when you get a demand.

Here are five easy steps to start in case you have considered meandering into a drop shipping business.

1. Open account on Amazon as a Seller.

The main move to make when starting drop shipping business is to open an account on Amazon as a seller. There are two sorts of reports that you can begin: Professional and individual consideration. In case you are starting and not sure of moving more than 40 products in a multi-month, it is proposed that you go for the Individual account. Regardless, it is essential you know the points of interest and disservices of any account you are settling on.

Here are favorable circumstances and burdens to oversee you in settling on the decision on which account to consent to acknowledge:

For Individual Account:

You are not allowed to use outcast services like Repricers and Inventory Lab. You have not met all prerequisites to list your product in the Buy Box. You can't make a distinction to register your product in limited categories of Amazon stores. There is $0.99 cost per item solds.

For Professional Account:

You can make use of a spreadsheet to exchange diverse items immediately utilizing the seller central. You will approach more reports on the seller board. You are possesse all the necessary qualities to list your product in the Buy Box. You can apply to register your products in restricted categories. You will pay $40 month to month cost notwithstanding the $0.99 charge per item sold. You can collect new product pages for your products.

Note that you can refresh your account at whatever point.

2. Find the best insignificant exertion drop ship suppliers.

Most drop shippers make good advantage using the best platform-Salehoo, to find impeccable drop shippers for products that they hope to move.

To start, join to paid Salehoo account to use their best gadgets and features. Search for drop shippers closes you that can ship snappier with lesser shipping costs.

Why it is fitting to use this platform is because, most suppliers don't have a spending plan for electronic life marketing. Instead they pass on the marketing costs over to cut down product costs. Like this, they'd lean toward buying into Salehoo than doing Google marketing.

Near it will require more effort on the suppliers' part to make an advance with PPC marketing, so they slant toward a submitted platform for it.

3. Search for negligible exertion yet high-moving products.

When you find a supplier that suits your subtleties, look through his/her list to discover those items that are not exorbitant but instead are in a like manner moving to a high degree well. Assurance that the esteem refinement between what is offered for that item on Amazon and what the supplier is putting forth is adequately enormous to make you some advantage.

Despite whether you decide to hotspot for sellers outside the Salehoo platform, the most fundamental thing is that there is advantage enough to deal with for cost in time and money.

4. Make an especially bare essential and search engine enhanced titles and delineations on Amazon.

Since you are set up with your products, keep on listing them on your Amazon store. Assurance you form SEO product depictions to enable your products to rank high on Amazon search result.

5. Just ahead and start marketing your products using differing propelled marketing system.

You can re-fitting the marketing to specialists on a platform like Fiverr.

HOW TO BE YOUR BOSS AS AN AMAZON FBA SELLER

It's each advanced workers want to create automated revenue streams, and to gain a pay by doings as messenger as could reasonably be expected.

This has driven numerous youthful business people to offshoot showcasing, or into the universe of e-stores and outsourcing. Some have succeeded, and most have not.

The Amazon commercial center is all the time neglected and gives a lot of opportunity to a first automated revenue stream.

The FBA benefit deals with the rest. Your product is set in perspective of Amazon's galactic commercial center. The item that you send to Amazon are put away in their distribution centers. At the point when a deal is made, they convey your question and even deal with client benefit.

It doesn't get considerably more inactive than that, yet before your fantasies get as well wild, this is no get-fast rich plan. To succeed, you should plug a decent couple of long stretches of diligent work into the endeavor.

The vast majority of your info will include researching

products to move and discovering providers who can give you the right price.

To buy the products, you will likewise require some startup capital.

The underlying sum that you contribute is altogether your decision. You can stock a product in your price go, and a measure of products that you can manage.

If you do your researchs and buy and move the right products at the right prices, you will be prepared to make deals and profits in the blink of an eye by any stretch of the imagination.

Cost To Start Selling

This isn't outsourcing. Before you start selling on FBA, you should have some money to contribute.

You should manage the buy of physical stock, and afterward, pay to send these items to Amazon. Buying from providers, and after that dispatching, the products to Amazon will be your primary costs.

When you have recorded a product, you can utilize the FBA number cruncher to work out the correct costs of these administration fees, as indicated by your product's value, deal price, and delivering values.

The real measure of money that you contribute is

altogether up to you. You could buy ten products for $50 each, or 1000 products for $100 each, or whatever you need or can manage. You are new to the diversion, and don't have much money to save, it is impeccably fine to start little and scale up later.

You never contribute beyond what you can bear to lose, and dependably choose products dependent on appropriate research, at that point there isn't so much hazard, and profits are likely.

Which Subscription Fee Is Best?

When you come to buy into FBA (secured soon), how would you know which subscription fee is best for you?

Everything relies upon what number of exchanges you make.

The primary plan enables you to offer up to 40 products in a multi-month, at a charge of $0.99 per item exchange. This could be the best alternative if you are dunking your toes in the water out of the blue, or you move expensive products, however, less of them. You plan to run under 40 products in a multi-month, choose this alternative.

You are probably going to make more than 40 exchanges, you should pay $39.99 for the month to month join. You need to quit fooling around and move several products, this is by a wide margin the best esteem. It likewise accompanies more highlights, for example, the capacity to charge deals impose, and produce business reports.

Joining To FBA

OK, this is it! You are sold on the possibility of FBA, and you comprehend that you need to put in some work to make it occur. You are about prepared to chase some bargain products that will move like hotcakes.

To start with, we should get you joined.

This is an obvious process:

Make a beeline for sellercentral.amazon.com

Enroll utilizing your current Amazon account, or make another one.

Choose your subscription plan dependent on what number of products you plan to move.

Express the legitimate name of your organization. You don't have an organization name, utilize your full name.

Give your Visa subtleties. This is in case your account encounters a shortage. This would occur on the off chance that you didn't offer any items yet at the same time needed to pay subscription and distribution center fees.

Choose your showcase name. This name is a piece of your image. Your clients need to identify with it, or if nothing else be outraged by it. Pick painstakingly. If you plan to move in a specific specialty, choose a significant name.

Next, you will be requested to confirm your character. This should be possible through a fast telephone call, or by instant message. You would then be able to finish your enlistment, and you will be an Amazon Seller. Cheerful days!

Presently you can enter your ledger subtleties, with the goal that Amazon can store your profits straight into your account. Go to 'Settings' > 'Account Info' and afterward look down to include a store method.

You should check your managing an account data before you can get payments.

Presently you are joined as an Amazon Seller, yet the last advance is to enlist for FBA.

Make a beeline for the FBA enlistment page, click 'Begin,' and you can without much of a stretch add FBA to your seller's account. You should merely peruse the T&C and after that concur.

Before you go any further, you require something to move. We're not doing this so you can get out your carport. We need to make a pleasant measure of money, with an average product supplied and prepared to move.

Finding The Right Product

Method 1 - Wholesalers

The primary method is the 'product first' approach. You will chase for bargain products, and after that contrast them with the Amazon postings to perceive how well they are probably going to move, and the amount they will run for.

This is a fundamental method, however not the one that can give the most high-profit edges. Successfully, you are watchful for chances to buy products at a decreased discount esteem, and after that rundown them on Amazon FBA.

This is one of the least complex method accessible for discovering products that are modest and can get a profit. You should merely waitlist your possibilities and after that research the Amazon prices.

You don't need to constrains yourself to the enormous box stores referenced previously. For more guidance on discovering wholesalers read this book.

Let's assume you locate a cell phone from Walmart, and it has a markdown offer. It appears to be shoddy. Checks Amazon and see that you can get the telephone for extensively short of what it is being advertised. You know that it has a high positioning (on the Amazon Best Seller's rundown), and is selling high. That would be a potential champ, and an opportunity to make money utilizing FBA.

Make beyond any doubt you generally consider the FBA fees when you are thinking about your products.

You must have the capacity to buy the products, dispatch them to Amazon, pay the fees, and still take a fair cut for yourself. A brilliant opportunity like that is uncommon, yet it does occur, and when it does you are in for a smooth ride!

There are impediments to this method. Although it is the most latent process, it very well may be hard to locate the right product. There can be a great deal of sticking around, and edges are generally thin.

You need to amplify your opportunity for profits, the time has come to remove the distributor, and go directly to the provider!

Methods 2 – Suppliers

This strategy is significantly more all out and requires a more noteworthy measure of contribution from you, yet whenever done right you can source products at a much lower cost, leaving you significantly more space for profit.

To expand potential, you would private be able to label products and move them as your own.

This may sound alarming; however, it's truly not too terrible. It's a doddle on the off chance that you will invest the underlying energy.

What Is Private Label Products?

A private label products is one that you can move under your brand.

You can purchase a lot of a specific product straightforwardly from a supplier. At that point, you can have the product branded with your labeling and bundling, and adequately advertise the product as though your very own organization supplies it.

Step 1: Take To The Bestsellers List

The best beginning stage for your examination is the Amazon Best Sellers list. It makes life extremely simple. The blockbusters list is designed for clients to have the capacity to perceive what is prevalent; however it additionally offers you the chance to see initially what as of now moves wells.

The lower the numbers (closer to #1), the higher the product is positioned inside its category. Rankings esteem are concerning the expansiveness of the group. A rate of #400 would be pretty good in a general group like 'Kitchen and Home,' and not very great in an extremely tight specialty category like 'Scented Oils.'

A positioning of underneath #1000 in a general category is commonly viewed as pretty good, and it implies a specific product is selling high.

What would you be able to take from that? The best and base of it is, you require a product that will move quick.

You can source the best selling product at a decent price, you get the opportunity to profit.

Step 2 – Narrow Down Your Options

Looking through the Best Seller list could abandon you with several potential options for FBA selling. It's an excellent opportunity to begin narrowing down your hunt. The initial step is to ignore any product that is unrealistic.

Most importantly, it might be ideal if the product can be lightweight. This can make postage, bundling, and storage less expensive. Little light protests that bring a decent price offer the best an incentive for transportation expenses and room.

More excellent articles ought not to be discounted, but instead, they ought to be essential and sufficiently profitable that the additional delivery and storage costs will be justified, despite all the trouble.

Your product ought to likewise be conventional.

This is a standout amongst the most vitals contemplations. Why? Consider it. If you find top selling Nike shoes, it's outlandish that you will have the capacity to move these as a private label – i.e., as your product. You would be sued instantly.

Moreover, the product could be a bestseller entirely because it is a Nike brand. You may have the capacity to find a supplier of nonexclusive shoes and bundle them up; however this doesn't mean you will accomplish indistinguishable statures from a setup brand.

Your most logical option, for reasonableness and sales, is to find a product that moves well for the real product itself, and one that could be branded and sold by you.

Step 3 - Research Your Competition

You will be left with a cluster of products that are selling admirably, and that are appropriate for your beautiful self to move on Amazon.

For every one of your potential products, make a note of the accompanying, utilizing a spreadsheet:

Product – The name of the product.

Hit rank – Should be beneath #1000

Price of listing: If a bestselling item looks extravagant, at that point you may have the capacity to match or undercut the price by finding the correct supplier.

The number of reviews – If a product is a 'Blockbuster', yet has a low number of studies, at that point, this recommends the market isn't yet immersed, and you might have the capacity to slip in addition to that your product. Then again, a product with several reviews may be hard to rival. This doesn't mean you should preclude an open door for profit; however, you ought to think about the quality of your opposition.

Any negative client reviews – Reviews could uncover product imperfections. Do clients have any grievances to make about the product? It's extraordinary news to be sure if a smash hit still has the opportunity to get better, or if negative reviews discolor their notoriety. Might you be able to give the client what they need with your product?

The nature of the listing – This isn't generally a central point, yet again it's only one approach to assist you with competing. If a high positioning product has an average or poor product portrayal, you might have the capacity to give a similar product, however, utilize an upgraded and all the more captivating sales pitch to commute home a few sales.

From this information, you ought to have the capacity to work out generally what your best options are. Furnish with this spreadsheet of shortlisted possibilities for your FBA sales; the time has come to contacts the suppliers and see what you can get at the correct cost.

Step 4 – Contact Suppliers

Kindly, don't flee in dread at the possibility of this. Reaching a supplier is similarly as simple as utilizing some other administration. This is particularly evident when you realize where to look.

You have nearby suppliers, companions in high places, or some other traps up to your sleeve, at that point directly ahead and work with what you have. For every other person, there is no excellent place over Alibaba, a worldwide stage for associating purchasers with suppliers.

On Alibaba (or whatever another stage that you favor), you can scan for the product that you shortlisted. Type the name of the product into the hunt box, and you will be demonstrated a fabulous list of suppliers who can offer what you are searching for.

This list will contain subtleties, for example, price ranges, product styles, and supplier's options for private labeling, and their base request amount (MOQ). Pick a supplier that appears to offer the best price for the style and amount of product that you are searching for.

You should contact the supplier specifically to get an immediate statement, for the most part by email.

Transaction

Try not to be reluctant to consult with the potential suppliers that you contact. Usually, they will need to make the sale, and you will have different options accessible.

You should as of now have a thought of how shoddy you have to source your products to rival comparative items and make a clean profit. Be sure, and willing to leave if a supplier can't descend on price.

It can converse with a few suppliers on the double, to ensure you can get the best price as well as the best quality product.

You are likewise very much qualified for demand an example to check whether the product is doing scratch.

This is profoundly prescribed. A shabby and defective item will before long feel the anger of Amazon reviewers and sink your expectations of profits. Ensure you are selling quality goods.

Step 5 – Design and Packaging (Private Label Only)

If you are purchasing products from a supplier who permits private label, you should send your designs for bundling, logos, and names.

Except if you are an expert visual designer, at that point, it's an excellent opportunity to bring in the specialists.

You don't need to burn up available resources balance. You can utilize independent stages like Upwork and Fiverr.com to find extraordinary esteem administrations.

The amount you spend relies on your financial plan.

If you can bear the cost, endeavor to sprinkle out a little on this underlying design stages, as expert branding could truly separate you as a seller.

When you have the completed design records, you can directly ahead and send them over to your supplier, with clear directions on the best way to continue.

Adding Your Products To Your Inventory

It will take possibly 14 days for your products to land from your supplier, maybe significantly more. Meanwhile, you can add your products to your FBA inventory.

This is an exceptionally straightforward process:

Sign in to your Seller Central record.

Snap 'Inventory' → 'Oversee Inventory'

Pick the 'Include a product' option.

Look for your product in the Amazon listings, utilizing the product name or the UPC, ISBN, EAN, or ASIN.

Ensure you pick the right product, style, and shading to coordinate the product that you found in the Best Sellers list.

(If you are conveying a brand new product to the commercial center, click 'It's not in the Amazon list' and adhere to directions. This isn't probably going to be the situation with the FBA selling strategies referenced here and is more applicable for producers.)

Next, click 'I need Amazon to dispatch and give client benefit,' to ensure FBA secures your products.

When you are done, tap the 'Spare and Finish' option.

Rehash this for all products that you intend to move on Amazon.

The inventory items will show up close to including them. You will see that their status is sets to 'dormant'. This will change once you have conveyed the products to Amazon.

Transportation Your Products

When your items touch base from your wholesaler or producer, the time has come to have them transported. Amazon makes this simple for you.

Keep in mind your inventory list, brimming with hidden items? This is the ideal opportunity to make them dynamic, by orchestrating their shipment:

Go to your inventory list.

Select at least one of the products that you need to ship to Amazon.

Snap 'Activities', and afterward select 'Send/Replenish Inventory' starting from the drop menu.

Create another shipment plan, affirm your location, and reveal to Amazon whether your products are individual or cased. Except if you got them from a maker, you would most likely select 'individual.'

Next, print your item marks. They coordinate your seller ID with your products, and ought to be set over the highest point of the first standardized tag. This is a prerequisite of FBA, so ensure you oblige. You can print them out on most sorts of a printer utilizing extraordinary sticky mark paper.

Affirm, and you will see your delivery subtleties. Check and endorse.

Choose your messenger. Except if you work with your messenger, you can utilize Amazon's accomplice UPS for household conveyances. You should locate your administration for universal sales.

After affirming, you will be provoked to enter the number of boxes you are sending, and the weight and measurements of the bundles. You will discover the price of your shipment now.

At long last, you should print your crate names. Once more, these match your shipment bundles with your Seller ID. One should be put on the highest point of each case.

You are working with your dispatch, enter their following number.

Affirm the shipment, and trust that the bundles will be gathered.

The most effective method to Make Sales

If you need to, you could consider it daily at present. Your product have been sourced at a rate that will acquire you some profit, and you have branded, marked, and delivered them off to Amazon. You will make a few sales, and you can watch the pay come in.

You may have figured out how to undermine the opposition on price, in which case the product may move. Nonetheless, you have a new brand name, and no customer reviews.

Promotion and appropriate advertising can never do any harm, and will more often than not bring you substantially more potential for profit.

You should need to help sales along, particularly in the beginning periods when your product may require somewhat of a push.

Making A Compelling Listing

First up, create your product listing. This is the thing that your potential customers will see when they tap on your item, so it should be right on the money.

Early introductions genuinely are everything.

Consider having the depiction composed by an expert if you figure it will help. You should include a lot of top-notch pictures to draw in purchasers.

You need to compose the portrayal yourself, you can likewise utilize headings (<h3></h3>), active content, (<b></b>), and visual cues (<li></li>) to make your substance more alluring. Seeing more about the Amazon product listing calculation will likewise help.

The way to a convincing product portrayal is to show what the product does, how it works, why it is significant, what separates it from others like it, and why it ought to be obtained immediately. Endeavor to cover these focuses in a drawing in tone, and a voice that addresses the product's intended interest group.

Keep in mind amid your exploration prior on when you took a gander at contender's listings?

What was absent?

What made some of them terrible?

What made the great ones emerge from the group?

Presently is your opportunity to move the product truly, and you need to benefit as much as possible from that possibility.

Create a perfect sales work of art!

Showcasing and Promotion

Price-Reduction

A standout amongst other approaches to give your product the push it needs is to begin off with a promotion, which could incorporate a markdown rate. If you are the new kid on the square, for what reason should a customer choose you? They will likely observe your product as a bad buy.

If you offer a rebate, you will decrease this apparent hazard, and increment the shot of making those critical initial couple of sales. Your product ends up being great; you can expect charmed reviews from customers.

You may need to endure an underlying shot to your profit edges if you make a price decrease; however it will be well justified, despite all the trouble to see a lift in your rankings, reviews, and brand identity.

Publicizing/PPC

Amazon offers a flexible interior publicizing framework that will keep your product high in significant hunts, and increment your permeability drastically. You can choose whatever spending you need for the campaign, from $100 upwards.

When you have picked up more solid notoriety, you shouldn't proceed with your campaign. Your sales positioning will increment, and you will show up usually higher up in quests. With even only a couple of customer reviews, you can gain the validity that can drive sales.

You can likewise utilize Google Adwords comparatively, to pick up permeability and sales. This will, in general, be more costly; however you can contact a group of people outside of Amazon, and this can be to a high degree compelling.

Web-based life Marketing

You plan on making a long haul brand that spends significant time in a particular kind of product, at that point you ought to consider assembling an internet-based life campaign that objectives your specialty. Create profile and pages for your business, or individual products, and do what you can to share them around.

You can likewise pay for web-based life promoting, like Facebook and Twitter, all together that your posts contact more individuals.

Post your product on important gatherings, discussions, web journals, and anyplace you can on the web.

Scaling Your Business

You need to begin little with regards to Amazon FBA selling. You would prefer not to directly ahead and contribute your life-funds purchasing the highest number of products from your provider as you could bear. You need to buy a sensible bunch of something reasonable, deliver it, move it, and profit.

There are numerous manners by which you could keep on scaling up your business. Here a few hints that will assist you with advancing an FBA seller:

Take the profit that you make from your first inventory stock, and reinvest it. Purchase business as a standard item and restock with a more prominent sum.

A specific product appears to work well for you and turns a decent profit rapidly, stay with it. Any of your products battle, or don't profit as you expected, at that point drop them from your stock list.

You began with extremely modest products; you could start to stock more costly choices as your business develops. This may enable you to capture more profit per sale and generally bring down transportation costs. While including products, you ought to dependably rehash the exploration stages completely.

Consider selling your product outside of Amazon. When your brand is set up on the Amazon seller circuit, why not take it further with your site, full internet-based life channels, videos, pictures, and e-stores? The online world is your clam!

Amazon FBA selling is no a get-fast rich plan. You realize that at this point. You additionally realize how much potential there is to make a profit. This is the genuine book for the individuals who will put the work in.

The procedure is genuinely clear. Your fundamental concern ought to research and finding the correct products. If you will do that and do it well, you will probably be compensated pleasantly.

CHAPTER SEVEN

HOW TO MAKE PASSIVE INCOME FROM AMAZON

When you realize how to make passive income from Amazon, there is no restriction to the amount of money that you can create.

Amazon is one of the least demanding on the web business models to make passive income from. Its stage has a great many clients from which you can take advantage of.

For whatever length of time that you keep up this income-delivering machine, it will keep on creating money for you. You've any point had a craving for working for yourself and ending up fiscally free, Amazon is your ticket to do as such.

It is safe to says that you are prepared to figure out how to make passive income from Amazon?

Amazon is outstanding amongst other passive income openings.

Outsider Amazon sales represent millions in sales every year, demonstrating that Amazon is an extraordinary method to sell products without managing the sales, the delivery, or the clients. Your

151

product does well; Amazon will advance it for you. They will rank it higher up in their web index, in this manner driving more sales to your page. This is one of the numerous reason why Amazon is the best place to begin selling products.

Passive income enables you to make money while you rest.

Suppose that you develop your Amazon product, and it's creation you significant money. In any case, following a year you choose to quit working on it. If you aren't proactively developing and keeping up your Amazon business, it might stagnate or gradually decrease and drop. This is the reason Amazon FBA isn't for everybody.

First and first phases of your business, you have to focus on taking every necessary step to manufacture and look after it. When you've done this, your business begins to work without you.

Think about an Amazon business as though it were a seed that you are planting in the ground. It won't become medium-term since this isn't a make easy money business. You need to water that seed and put in the work to develop it. As you are watering your seed, some things are going on under the ground that you can't see.

There is a solid establishment that is being fabricated that will support your future achievement. If you experience the procedure and are reliable with it, that seed will begin to grow. As you keep on supporting the development of your business, in the long run, it will end up being a tree that never again requires the upkeep that it once did. Now it will accommodate you, long haul, eventually prompting money related opportunity.

This is the means by which to make passive income from Amazon.

The excellence of Amazon is that they genuinely deal with the majority of the substantial liftings for you. Be that as it may, you must take every necessary step, in advance, to receive the benefits.

AMAZON FBA – PASSIVE INCOME?

Passive income as money earned by not specifically exchanging time for a predefined amount of money (like with an hourly or pay paid employments).

For situation, we are doing the retail exchange variant of the business. We invest energy forthright hunting down arrangement. We purchases as much as we can amid each shopping excursion. We at that point set up the items and ship them to Amazon. We spend a couple of hours every weeks doing exercises. 2 or 3 hours shopping and an additionals 2 hours to get the stuff prepared and sent. A few weeks we shop somewhat more, and a few weeks we don't buy by any stretch of the imagination.

In the wake of doing those things, everything we do is kick back and trust that the sales will occur and believe that the money will come in.

CONCLUSION

FBA is a process whereby Amazon stocks a seller's goods and record available to be purchased at their site, and additionally taking installment for requests and conveying products to buyers. Amazon FBA is a business opportunity given by Amazon to urge business-proprietors to list their products in its marketplace.

Since you can deal with stock on the webs. You send your product to Amazon, and after that, you transfer your listings to Seller Central. Your products are recorded in your Amazon record, and you can change over them to an FBA listing.

Pick Amazon's limited shipping or assign your transporter so that customers can order your product. Customers will order your product and Amazon will ship it to them, giving the following data.

Begin with Fulfillment by Amazon and let Amazon deal with the subtleties while you maintain your business. Making money selling on Amazon is generally straightforward. Recognizing what clients are searching for in a product is an integral part of being a fruitful Amazon salesperson. Each seller ought to have the most extreme respectability and trustworthiness in all sales that they do.

Go on and give it a go, you don't have anything to lose and a lot to pick up. You pursue the majority of the means and guidance contained in this book, at that point, you can make a pleasant measure of automated revenue as an Amazon FBA seller. Appreciate!

CPSIA information can be obtained
at www.ICGtesting.com
Printed in the USA
LVHW011134240921
698651LV00003B/307